Are the World's Coral Reefs Threatened?

Other books in the At Issue series:

Affirmative Action
Are Efforts to Reduce Terrorism Successful?
Club Drugs
Do Animals Have Rights?
Does the World Hate the United States?
Do Infectious Diseases Pose a Serious Threat?
Do Nuclear Weapons Pose a Serious Threat?
The Ethics of Capital Punishment
The Ethics of Euthanasia
The Ethics of Genetic Engineering
The Ethics of Human Cloning
Fast Food
Food Safety
Gay and Lesbian Families
Gay Marriage
Gene Therapy
How Can School Violence Be Prevented?
How Should America's Wilderness Be Managed?
How Should the United States Withdraw from Iraq?
Internet Piracy
Is Air Pollution a Serious Threat to Health?
Is America Helping Afghanistan?
Is Gun Ownership a Right?
Is North Korea a Global Threat?
Is Racism a Serious Problem?
The Israeli-Palestinian Conflict
Media Bias
The Peace Movement
Reproductive Technology
Sex Education
Should Juveniles Be Tried as Adults?
Teen Suicide
Treating the Mentally Ill
UFOs
What Energy Sources Should Be Pursued?
What Motivates Suicide Bombers?
Women in the Military

Are the World's Coral Reefs Threatened?

Charlene Ferguson, *Book Editor*

Bruce Glassman, *Vice President*
Bonnie Szumski, *Publisher*
Helen Cothran, *Managing Editor*

GREENHAVEN PRESS
An imprint of Thomson Gale, a part of The Thomson Corporation

Detroit • New York • San Francisco • San Diego • New Haven, Conn.
Waterville, Maine • London • Munich

For more information, contact
Greenhaven Press
27500 Drake Rd.
Farmington Hills, MI 48331-3535
Or you can visit our Internet site at http://www.gale.com

LIBRARY OF CONGRESS CATALOGING-IN-PUBLICATION DATA

Are the world's coral reefs threatened? / Charlene Ferguson, book editor.
    p. cm. — (At issue)
Includes bibliographical references and index.
ISBN 0-7377-2697-0 (lib. : alk. paper) — ISBN 0-7377-2698-9 (pbk. : alk. paper)
    1. Coral reef ecology. 2. Endangered ecosystems. 3. Nature—Effect of human beings on. I. Ferguson, Charlene. II. At issue (San Diego, Calif.)
QH541.5.C7A74 2005
333.95'22—dc22
                                                  2004053918

Contents

Page

Introduction   7

1. The World's Coral Reefs Are Threatened   10
   Franklin Moore and Barbara Best

2. The Threat to Some Coral Reefs Is Exaggerated   19
   Rachel Nowak

3. Global Warming Causes Coral Bleaching   26
   Ove Hoegh-Guldberg

4. Global Warming Does Not Cause Coral Bleaching   33
   Sallie Baliunas and Willie Soon

5. Coral Reefs Face Many Natural and Human Threats   39
   Brian J. English

6. Cyanide Fishing Threatens Coral Reefs   48
   Charles Victor Barbor and Vaughan R. Pratt

7. African Dust May Threaten Coral Reefs   56
   John C. Ryan

8. Tourism Threatens Coral Reefs   65
   United Nations Environment Programme

9. Trade in Coral Organisms Threatens Coral Reefs   69
   Andrew W. Bruckner

10. Fishing Bans to Protect Coral Reefs Should Be Expanded   77
    Keay Davidson

11. Fishing and Boating Bans May Not Protect Coral Reefs   81
    Ryck Lydecker

12. Satellite Imaging Helps Scientists Study Threatened Coral Reefs   86
    Brian Soliday

13. Artificial Coral Reefs May Save Coral Ecosystems   93
      from Extinction
        Caspar Henderson

Organizations to Contact   99

Bibliography   104

Index   107

Introduction

Coral reefs have existed for more than a hundred million years. Known as the rain forests of the sea, they are one of the oldest ecosystems on earth. Coral reefs cover less than two-tenths of a percent of the ocean floor but contain approximately 25 percent of the oceans' species. So far, approximately five thousand species of reef fish and more than twenty-five hundred species of coral have been identified. Those species thus far indentified make up less than 10 percent of coral biodiversity and scientists estimate that another 1 to 8 million coral reef species have yet to be discovered.

Coral reefs are like a bustling city beneath the sea. For generations millions of tiny, fragile animals called coral polyps, spineless animals, have formed colonies. When these polyps die, the leave their skeletons of calcium carbonate behind, creating reefs of limestone. These massive reefs are multistory structures with holes and crevices that are home to millions of animals and plants. A multitude of marine organisms take up residency in the reefs. The juveniles become firmly attached to the reef and are unable to leave. To compensate for this immobility, the reef dwellers produce and secrete complex chemical agents that allow them to catch their prey, protect themselves from predators, avoid disease, and attract mates. These powerful chemicals are among the compounds that scientists are now researching to find new life-sustaining medicinal cures.

Before looking to coral reefs, those who developed medicinal drugs relied on a variety of sources. Forty to 50 percent of the medicinal drugs currently used have been developed in the last twenty to thirty years and are derived from natural sources such as terrestrial flora (plants) and fauna (animals). "Most [medicinal drugs] are from tropical rain forests, and 95 percent [of the forests] have been studied," says Tom Collins, academic affairs chief for Scripps Institution of Oceanography in San Diego, California. "So the disease fighting drug potential of the forests and other areas has about run out." For this reason, some scientists see the ocean as a virtual treasure chest of potential medicines, as only 5 percent of known ocean resources have been studied. "The prospect of finding a new drug in the sea, especially among coral reef species, may be three hundred to four hundred times more likely than isolating one from a terrestrial ecosystem," Andrew Baker, a coral reef ecologist, states.

Some researchers have already taken advantage of the coral reefs' potential as medicine. For years coral has been used for bone grafts, and other coral reef ecosystem resources have been used in both medicinal and cosmetic skin-care products. For example, the drug AZT, used in the fight against AIDS, was based on compounds extracted from a Caribbean reef sponge. A chemical called kainic acid has been found in Japan's coral reefs. Kainic acid is being used as a diagnostic chemical to investigate Huntington's chorea, a rare nerve disease that is fatal. The Japanese have also isolated a substance from a soft coral, *Sarcophyton glaucum*, that can inhibit the development of skin cancer. The substance has proved to reduce cancer in mice, but further tests and human trials are needed to draw final conclusions about its effectiveness in humans. While diving on Bennett's Shoal off the coast of Australia, marine chemistry professor William Fenical of Scripps Institution of Oceanography discovered *Eleutherobia*, a rare species of yellow coral. This coral produces a chemical known as eleutherobin, which works like Taxol, a chemotherapy drug, and could be a new weapon against breast and ovarian cancers. Fenical contends, "Everybody is saying we need new antibiotics, where are we going to get them? And here is this vast resource out there in the ocean that has been completely overlooked despite the fact that the oceans form the majority of the surface on the earth." Researchers at Florida Atlantic University found that the enzyme secosteroids, a chemical defense mechanism that corals use to fight their own diseases, can work in a similar way in humans. This enzyme is now being used to treat asthma, arthritis, and inflammatory disorders, and is also being used to control tumor growth.

One of the impediments to the research potential of coral reef medicines in the past was the lack of accessibility and the enormous financial cost associated with obtaining them. However, the latest evolving technology in diving equipment, from remote-operated underwater vehicles to undersea research laboratories, has given scientists new opportunities for further exploration. According to coral reef ecologist Andrew Baker, "The United States and other countries are only beginning to invest in marine biotechnology." Baker is not concerned about the financial challenges of obtaining coral reef medicines. "Even with limited funding, U.S. marine biotechnology efforts since 1983 have resulted in more than 170 U.S. patents, with close to 100 new compounds patented between 1996 and 1999. U.S. support for marine biotechnology research is likely to increase in the coming years." Funding from nongovernmental sources, such as the National Cancer Institute (NCI) and universities, is increasing. According to the National Oceanic and Atmospheric Administration (NOAA), marine biotechnology has become a multibillion-dollar industry worldwide, with a projected annual growth rate of 15 to 20 percent during the next five years. Now more than half of all new cancer drug research focuses on marine organisms.

Research shows that the coral reef ecosystem is a proven source of medicinal cures that can combat disease. Currently over six thousand unique chemical compounds have been isolated from marine organisms that either live in, or depend on, the coral reefs for their survival, with many more yet to be discovered. Every day researchers are finding new life-saving cures from the coral reef ecosystem that can help sustain and give humankind a better quality of life. Thus, some scientists claim that coral reefs are the key to humanity's future. As a result, scientists are concerned by potential threats to this ecosystem and warn that the loss of biodiversity would have devastating effects on the discovery and development of new life-sustaining medicines. Such threats include overfishing, which upsets the ecosystem on which coral reefs depend, coastal construction, which suffocates the reef in sediment; tourism, which disrupts and exploits reef life; and coral bleaching, which some claim is a result of global warming. Understanding the nature and scope of the threat to coral reefs is important to those who hope to tap the reefs' medicinal potential.

1

The World's Coral Reefs Are Threatened

Franklin Moore and Barbara Best

Franklin Moore is acting director for environment and acting deputy assistant administrator at the U.S. Agency for International Development (USAID), an independent federal agency that provides economic and humanitarian assistance worldwide. Barbara Best, a professor of marine biology, is coastal resource and policy adviser for environment for USAID.

Coral reefs, among the most valuable and diverse of the world's ecosystems, are found along the coasts of over one hundred countries. Reefs are a source of food, medicinal drugs, recreation, and tourism. They are also home to millions of species of animals and plants, and they protect shorelines from waves and storms. Unfortunately, overfishing, pollution, and global warming pose significant threats to coral reefs worldwide. In addition, removal of coral and ornamental coral reef fish for use in aquariums reduces the coral habitat. Although the United States has laws to protect its reefs, it imports coral reef products from nations that do not, thus contributing to coral reef decline. As an international trade leader, the United States must discourage the use of destructive practices and reward responsible use of these precious resources.

B y any measure, coral reefs are among the most diverse and valuable ecosystems on earth. Coral reefs occur in over 100 countries, most of them developing countries without the capacity or financial resources to adequately manage these vital resources. Reefs support at least a million described species of animals and plants, and another 8 million coral reef species are estimated to be as yet undiscovered.

According to one estimate, coral reefs provide goods and services worth about $375 billion each year—a staggering figure for an ecosystem which covers less than one percent of the earth's surface. Reef systems provide economic and environmental services to millions of people as shoreline protection from waves and storms, as places for recreation and tourism, and as sources of food, pharmaceuticals, livelihoods, and revenues.

In developing countries, coral reefs contribute about one-quarter of the total fish catch, providing food to an estimated one billion people in Asia alone. Globally, half a billion people are estimated to live within 100 kilometers of a coral reef and benefit from its production and protection. In light of expected climate change and associated sea level rises, coral reefs can offer a natural, self-building and self-repairing breakwater against wave and storm damage. These extremely valuable ecosystems constitute the economic base and future hope for sustained development in many countries, particularly small island nations.

Coral reefs in crisis

A . . . report from the Global Coral Reef Monitoring Network estimates that 25% of the world's reefs are already gone or severely damaged and that another third are degraded and threatened. This coral reef crisis is happening here at home in the U.S. and in far away places, in some of the most remote areas of the world.

Coral reefs are in serious trouble worldwide from a powerful combination of stresses that are threatening their survival, including:

- overexploitation of resources for subsistence and commercial fishing;
- destructive fishing practices, that degrade and destroy the habitat itself;
- increasing coastal populations, which are expected to double in the next 50 years;
- poor land use practices and runoff of pollutants, sediments and nutrients;
- disease outbreaks, which may be associated with poor water quality and pollutants;

- coral bleaching, associated with increasing seawater temperatures and global change; and
- removal of coastal mangrove forests.

These direct and indirect human activities pose significant threats to coral reef ecosystems, and the human populations that depend on them, particularly small island developing countries. For example:

- In northern Jamaica, it is estimated that almost all of the reefs are dead or severely degraded from overfishing and coastal runoff. Fish stocks have declined to a point where local fishers are now straining fish larvae out of the sea for fish soup.
- Philippines, degraded reefs and fish populations have led to an 18% decrease in the amount of protein in the average diet.

Human impacts are also occurring on U.S. reefs, oftentimes for use as luxury items. For example, in Hawaii at Honaunau, the top ten aquarium fish species have decreased by 59% over the last 20 years, and at Kona the most popular aquarium fish show declines in abundance from 38 to 57%.

> *Coral reefs provide goods and services worth about $375 billion each year—a staggering figure for an ecosystem which covers less than one percent of the earth's surface.*

Even under ideal conditions, it would take more than a lifetime for some reefs to recover. We can no longer continue to take coral reefs or mangrove forests for granted, or to assume that they can support unlimited resource use or unmanaged global trade.

Mangrove forests and coral reefs in trouble

While coral bleaching may be one of the largest threats facing coral reefs, international trade is having significant impacts on even the most remote and pristine reefs. Recent surveys of reefs worldwide found that many species of high commercial value were absent, or present in very low numbers, in almost all the reefs surveyed. Results suggest that almost all coral reefs have been affected by overfishing, and that there may be no pristine reefs left in the world.

International trade is also posing significant threats to mangrove forests, another critical coastal ecosystem that is intimately connected to coral reefs. Mangrove forests serve as important nurseries for many reef species. They help to maintain coastal water quality by reducing the run-off of sediments, pollutants, and excess nutrients from the land. Nutrients and energy flow between these habitats as species move between them.

In some areas of the world, the major loss of mangrove forests is due to the construction of shrimp mariculture ponds for the world market. The cheap shrimp we consume here in the U.S. comes with enormous ecological and social costs for the local communities where mariculture ponds are inappropriately sited and intensively farmed.

Driving destructive fishing practices

How does the international trade in wild coral reef animals and products more directly impact reefs? Primarily through overfishing and the use of destructive fishing practices. Live fish for both the food trade and marine ornamental trade are often caught with the use of cyanide or other poison, which temporarily stuns the fish for easy collection. Cyanide use is a serious threat to some of the world's richest coral reefs, as the cyanide kills corals and many other coral reef organisms. The lucrative and unregulated international trade in reef fishes drives the use of cyanide. It is estimated that since the 1960's, more than one million kilograms of cyanide has been squirted onto Philippine reefs alone, and the practice has spread throughout East Asia and the Indo-Pacific.

> *Even under ideal conditions, it would take more than a lifetime for some reefs to recover.*

Various explosives, such as dynamite and homemade bombs, are also used to kill fish for easy collection, but at an enormous cost to the reef, which is reduced to rubble. In Komodo National Park in Indonesia, about half of the reefs have already been destroyed through the use of explosives, forming beds of coral rubble that can extend several football fields in length. While the use of explosives to collect dead fish is usually for domestic trade, some of the fish that are only stunned will enter the international trade stream.

// Various explosives, such as dynamite and homemade bombs, are also used to kill fish for easy collection, but at an enormous cost to the reef, which is reduced to rubble. //

International trade is also driving the removal of the calcareous skeleton or base of the reef itself; reef skeletons are sold as "live rock" for marine aquaria. This base is the resulting accumulation of coral skeletons over tens to hundreds and thousands of years. Living coral, which constitutes the essential reef habitat for a myriad of species, is also collected and shipped live for marine aquaria, or killed and dried for the curio and shell trade.

The problem of overfishing

In addition to destructive practices, international trade is driving overfishing and the selected removal of key groups from coral reefs. Major groups targeted for trade are:
- groupers and wrasses for the live food fish trade;
- dead fish and invertebrates for food, medicinal products, and ornamentals including sharks, sea cucumbers, sea stars, mollusks and sea horses;
- live fish, coral and other invertebrates for marine aquaria and the ornamental hobby; and,
- "live rock" or the calcareous base of the reef for marine aquaria.

The marine ornamental trade for the pet industry often targets rare fish and coral species, as these can fetch the highest prices. The trade is also targeting large-polyped corals, which tend to be the slowest growing and the least common. By targeting the large groupers and wrasses, the live food fish trade removes key species from these ecosystems, thus altering their dynamics. The loss of some is comparable to the loss of major predators from terrestrial ecosystems. Other fishes feed on algae, and thus play an important role in ensuring that corals are not overgrown by more rapidly growing algae. The removal of coral for the marine aquarium trade and for use as curios and knickknacks, and the removal of the "live rock" base, reduces the essential reef habitat.

There are strong economic incentives associated with this international trade. The live food fish trade through Hong Kong alone is estimated to have a retail value of about one billion dollars a year. Some species of fish, selected live from a restaurant tank, can sell for almost $300 per plate. The global retail of marine ornamental fishes and aquarium hobby supplies is estimated at $500 million. Last year, for example, a pair of rare fish sold for over $5,000 each. Over 1000 different species of coral reef animals are now traded for marine aquaria.

The impacts from international trade are quite different from other more chronic causes of reef degradation, as these impacts are felt even in the most remote, pristine reefs. The use of destructive fishing practices, such as the use of cyanide, is spreading throughout the Indo-Pacific as fishing boats venture farther to find new unexploited fishing grounds.

> *Fish imported for the marine aquarium market . . . are captured with the use of cyanide and other poisons, which kills non-target animals and the coral reef itself.*

There is already strong international concern that some coral reef species are threatened or may become threatened through trade. Those species are listed under the Convention on the International Trade in Endangered Species of Wild Fauna and Flora (CITES), and include 2000 species of hard (stony) corals, black coral, giant clams, Queen conch, and sea turtles.

The consequences of destructive fishing practices

International trade is driving destructive fishing practices and unsustainable harvests from coral reef ecosystems, reducing the value of coral reefs to local communities and prospects for long term sustainable use. In some areas, depletion of stocks and the destruction of the reefs are threatening peoples' food security.

This international trade is a highly mobile trade; as stocks are depleted in one area or country, the trade moves on to other areas, often spreading the use of destructive fishing practices. Thus, the nature of the trade provides few incentives for long-term sustainable use by a community, and few benefits are channeled to the local communities.

The use of poisons and hooka gear can have serious consequences for the collectors themselves. Cyanide fishing poses human health risks to the fishers through exposure to the poison. A hooka rig is a low-tech approach to scuba diving that involves a compressor on the boat that pushes air down long tubes to divers below. Divers can spend many long hours under water collecting with hooka rigs. Unsafe diving practices by untrained divers can lead to the divers' "bends" and result in joint disease and even paralysis and death. Each week, several divers who have contracted the bends are taken by fishing boats in Honduras for treatment in the local diving decompression chamber. These divers have been collecting spiny lobsters to supply the growing U.S. appetite for seafood. Similar reports of injuries to divers come from South East Asian countries where hooka rigs are used for collecting marine ornamental fish and live food fish.

The U.S. role in international trade

In 1998, in response to the coral reef crisis, the Executive Order for the Protection of Coral Reefs was signed. The Order created the U.S. Coral Reef Task Force as a way of coordinating federal and state efforts, and charges federal agencies with the conservation and sustainable use of reef resources both domestically and worldwide. The Task Force was also asked to analyze and address the U.S. role in the international trade of coral and coral reef species.

The results of the trade analysis reveal that while live reef fish for the food fish market primarily go to Asian markets, the U.S. is the number one consumer of live coral and marine fishes for the aquarium trade and of coral skeletons and precious corals for curios and jewelry. Inadvertently, American consumers are contributing to the worldwide decline and degradation of reefs.

A closer examination of the U.S. trade reveals that the U.S. was consistently the largest importer of live coral during the

1990s, importing over 80% of the live coral and 95% of the live "rock" or reef base. Ironically, the U.S. prohibits the collection of coral and live rock in its own waters as they are considered essential fish habitats.

> *Other exploiters, whose primary interest is in making money without sharing benefits with local communities, should not be allowed to profit from these precious [coral reef] resources.*

In addition to coral, the United States imports nearly half (eight million) of the total worldwide trade in aquarium fishes (15–20 million/year). Many of the fish imported for the marine aquarium market in the U.S. are captured with the use of cyanide and other poisons, which kills non-target animals and the coral reef itself. Sustainability concerns will only increase with the growing international trade. The international trade in coral and live rock to supply the aquarium trade has increased at a rate of 12 to 30% per year since 1990.

The U.S. role in addressing the trade threat

The U.S. is part of the problem. The U.S. needs to be part of the answer. As a major consumer and importer of coral reef organisms, a major player in the world trade arena, and a leader in coral reef conservation efforts, the U.S. has a critical responsibility to not only address the degradation and loss of coral reef ecosystems worldwide, but to also encourage more responsible trade. As consumers, the U.S. should discourage the use of destructive or unsustainable collection practices that may jeopardize the future potential of coral reefs to sustain the local communities who depend on them for food and livelihoods. Rather, we should reward and encourage responsible use of these precious resources, and shift the burden of proof of sustainable use, for commercial and recreational purposes, to the users.

We need to emphasize community-based management of coral reef resources so that people living on and around coral reefs may share in the profits from coral reef activities. Other exploiters, whose primary interest is in making money without sharing benefits with local communities, should not be allowed to profit from these precious resources.

Oftentimes, local communities or national fisheries departments lack the capacity to sustainably manage reef resources, or to resist the short-term, high gain, economic incentives associated with the live food fish and marine ornamental trades. The U.S. Agency for International Development (USAID) is the principal agency of the U.S. Government responsible for building capacity in sustainable resource use in developing countries. USAID is . . . working with local communities and national governments in about 20 countries to assist them in conserving and managing their coral reef and coastal resources through capacity building for integrated coastal management, better land-use practices, sustainable fisheries management, and marine protected areas.

There are also immediate actions available to the U.S. public in terms of awareness and individual consumer choice. There is an urgent need to develop positive trade regimes so that only products from reefs under sustainable management plans are allowed into or out of the U.S., to ensure that consumer demand by Americans is not contributing to the decline and degradation of coral reefs.

We must change our view of how we treasure and value natural resources. For example, [in January 2001], the U.S. adopted new trade measures covering the import of antiquities from Italy into the U.S.; all antiquities from Italy must now be accompanied by documentation and certification as to how they were collected and where they are from, to ensure that they are from legitimate sources.

We must take a similar approach to natural resources. The U.S. government is promoting the idea among other nations within the Asia Pacific Economic Cooperation forum that consuming nations must bear some of the responsibility for their imports, and it is considering this approach for reef resources.

The U.S. could play a significant role by helping reward responsible practices, creating market incentives for responsible behaviors, and requiring certification of non-destructive collection practices and demonstration of sustainable collection of coral reef species. In this way, government, consumers, hobbyists and industry members can work together to ensure a responsible trade.

2

The Threat to Some Coral Reefs Is Exaggerated

Rachel Nowak

Rachel Nowak is a staff writer for New Scientist, *a science and technology newsmagazine.*

Some scientists and conservationists exaggerate the threat to Australia's Great Barrier Reef, one of the world's most diverse reef systems. Reports show that compared to reefs worldwide, the Great Barrier Reef is in good condition, but once spread by the media slight exaggerations sometimes turn into stories that the reef is dying. When scientists misrepresent the extent of the threat to coral reefs in order to force policy makers to discontinue detrimental farming practices or acknowledge the impact of global warming, they lose credibility. In consequence, real threats to the reefs are ignored. Proving that a threat such as agricultural runoff directly harms the reef is in fact difficult, but facts, not exaggerated fears, should determine decisions on how funds to protect the environment are spent.

The Great Barrier Reef is dying, crushed by an onslaught of rising ocean temperature, farming runoff, plagues of crown-of-thorns starfish, fishing and tourism. Better visit this rainforest of the oceans before it's too late. Right?

Wrong. Far from being on its last legs, the reef is in glowing health. Indeed, according to the 2002 "Report on the Status of the World's Coral Reefs," the reef is "predominantly in good condition," and just about pristine compared with reefs elsewhere in the world. So how has the perception that the reef is in imminent danger of collapse become entrenched in the public consciousness?

Distorting reef health

According to a small but increasingly vocal group of reef experts, the problem lies with scientists and conservation groups who have been distorting the health of the reef for their own ends, seeing this as a way of forcing politicians to ensure it is managed in an environmentally sound way, and making people take global climate issues seriously.

The experts agree that it would be no bad thing to tackle global warming . . . and Queensland's [Australia] intensive farming practices, which if nothing else are having a detrimental impact on state's terrestrial ecology. They even agree that coral reefs around the world have taken a terrible hammering. But, they say, those who use the Great Barrier Reef as a stick to beat governments and farmers with are putting scientific credibility at risk. And that will undermine other efforts to protect the reef from current and future threats.

"Imagine they develop an agrochemical that really does kill corals. The farmers are going to stand up and say, 'You said crown-of-thorns starfish and coral bleaching and sediment were killing the coral too.' We would have lost our credibility," says marine physicist Peter Ridd of James Cook University in Townsville, Queensland.

Not everyone agrees. "It's a fine line between overselling the problem and improper complacency," says Miles Furnas, an oceanographer at the Australian Institute of Marine Science (AIMS) in Townsville. If the reef is beginning to show the first signs of wear and tear, as many coral experts suspect, then it is vital to act now. "The dilemma of management means that if you wait long enough to see evidence of clear change, substantial damage has already occurred," he says.

An important reef

At 2000 kilometres long, the Great Barrier Reef is one of the most diverse reef systems in the world, accounting for almost one-fifth of the world's coral reefs. Add the fact that it's fabulously photogenic and has World Heritage Area status, and you can see why the reef is an icon for environmentalists everywhere.

So reports that sediment, nutrients and agrochemicals washed down from Queensland's sugar cane and cattle stations were wreaking havoc on the reef reverberated around the world, not least in articles published in [*New Scientist*]. On paper it doesn't look good. The Great Barrier Reef Marine Park Authority (MPA), the statutory body that manages the reef, asserts that over the past 150 years, sediment discharged from the mainland to the reef has increased by at least a factor of 3 and possibly a factor of 9, nitrogen by a factor of 2 to 4, and phosphate by a factor of between 3 and 15.

> *// Scientists and conservation groups . . . have been distorting the health of the reef for their own ends. //*

Worst still, pesticides such as Diuron have also been detected in sediments in the reef, it says. [In August 2002], a report containing those figures by a team of land-water and reef scientists helped nudge the Queensland state government and the federal government in Canberra into setting up a plan to deal with the problem.

Lacking direct evidence

But direct evidence that a problem actually exists is proving harder to come by. An extensive review in 2001 by ecologist David Williams of the Cooperative Research Centre for the Great Barrier Reef noted that only roughly a quarter of the inshore reefs, themselves a fraction of the whole reef system, are at risk even of "potential impacts." The report also acknowledged that establishing whether a reef has been damaged by agricultural run-off has proved nigh-on impossible for a variety of reasons, including frequent natural disturbances such as cyclones, and because monitoring has only been in place for the past 20 years or so. Williams nevertheless says there is cause for concern in circumstantial evidence, which suggests that at least some of the inner reefs are threatened by agricultural run-off.

Ridd agrees that agricultural run-off could in theory pose a threat, but he is categorical that it won't be due to sediment.

His studies have shown that any sediment from rivers is swamped by the amount lifted from the sea bottom by waves. More work needs to be done on pesticide and nutrient run-off to see if this is having an impact, but Ridd believes that ecologists and environmentalists tend to underestimate how much these pollutants are diluted once they reach the ocean. "Just because you can a show an increase in fertiliser use or detect pesticides in subtidal sediments, it doesn't mean that there's a problem. But it gets picked up by Greenpeace—and why shouldn't it be, when it's come from the Great Barrier Reef Marine Park Authority?" he says.

> **//** *Those who use the Great Barrier Reef as a stick to beat governments and farmers with are putting scientific credibility at risk.* **//**

Furnas is not reassured by these arguments. "We have never seen a reef in the Great Barrier Reef clobbered by nutrients or sediment. But what we are seeing—the low coral cover, and low diversity—is possibly the beginning of the process." That, combined with the unequivocal evidence that coral reefs from Hawaii to Hong Kong have been damaged by agricultural run-off, is reason enough to take action now. He accepts, however, that some scientists may have exaggerated the problem. "Science is a human endeavour, just like politics and journalism, and sometimes they put a spin on it."

The global warming debate

Even more disturbing, at first sight, than the threats of agricultural run-off are reports that global warming is killing the reef by bleaching coral. "Southern and central sites of the Great Barrier Reef are likely to be severely affected by sea temperature rise within the next 20 to 40 years," said Ove Hoegh-Guldberg, director of the Centre for Marine Studies at the University of Queensland, in a 1999 study commissioned by Greenpeace. The average sea temperature on the reef has increased by 0.3°C since the end of the 19th century, and huge tracts of the reef have certainly been bleached on two occasions in the past five years.

Corals bleach when they spit out the symbiotic algae that

they depend on to provide carbohydrates through photosynthesis. The favoured theory goes that when the sea is too warm, and conditions too sunny, the algae go into photosynthetic overdrive, spewing out so many dangerous free radicals that the coral are forced to eject them. If temperatures drop soon enough, the algae and coral happily reunite. But if the coral are deprived of their food source for too long they starve to death.

It's a compelling story. Indeed, of all the potential threats to the reef, this is the one on which there is most agreement. Nonetheless, in the rush to sound the alarm, the uncertainties about bleaching—a phenomenon that has been under the microscope for only four years or so—have been lost from the message. In 1998, 16 per cent of the world's reefs bleached. "The scientists took one look and thought they were dead. But what we are seeing is that about half the reefs that were severely damaged are recovering," says Clive Wilkinson, a coral reef expert at AIMS and editor of the "Report on the Status of World's Coral Reefs." Meanwhile, on the reef, the patterns of bleaching in the 2002 event were mysteriously different from the 1998 event, with some corals that were supposedly supersensitive to bleaching, such as the hard coral family Pocilloporidae, surviving well. "It's a real conundrum," says Wilkinson.

> *Coral experts understand far less about the threat posed by bleaching than conservation groups and some scientists like to suggest.*

None of this means that coral bleaching isn't cause for concern. It might subtly change the reefs' composition, even if it doesn't kill them. But coral experts understand far less about the threat posed by bleaching than conservation groups and some scientists like to suggest.

Spreading alarmist stories

Meanwhile, plagues of crown-of-thorns starfish, which suck the polyps out of coral skeleton, have descended on the reef three times since the 1960s, including the current outbreak. During each onslaught, coral experts have claimed that the reef won't recover. Yet so far it always has. Similar alarmist stories have circulated at different times that link overfishing, tourism and shipping damage to the demise of the reef.

But how have reports of potential and future threats to the ongoing health of the reef become twisted into perceptions that it is already dying? One reason may be the temptation to overstate the problems to win research dollars. "I've done it," says Ridd. "I would hate to look through my old grant proposals. We push the worst-case scenarios to show how important our research is."

> *Reports of potential and future threats to the ongoing health of the reef become twisted into perceptions that it is already dying.*

A slight exaggeration by scientists may get amplified once it has been passed on by the media and environmental groups like Greenpeace and WWF [World Wildlife Fund]. "It's the challenge of trying to sell the precautionary story," says Paul Marshall, manager of coral bleaching issues at the Great Barrier Reef MPA. "I try hard to distinguish between coral bleaching and coral dying," he insists. "But the whiteness looks so spectacular, and that's what the media runs with. The idea that white coral isn't necessarily dead gets lost."

One expert who admitted that the evidence is wanting, still told *New Scientist* he had a "gut feeling" that something is wrong with the reef. Sentiments like that, combined with the real passion many scientists feel for protecting the reef's future, may be all it takes to see the ambiguities dropped from the message.

Take a recent Great Barrier Reef MPA brochure on water quality—a distillation of the longer report that convinced the government to act on water quality on the reef. While detailing changing farming practices in Queensland, and the devastation wreaked by agriculture on reefs in other parts of the world, it fails to mention that there is no direct evidence of any damage to the reef, and that only small areas are even under threat. While not exactly inaccurate, says Ridd, the brochure and the report, which is posted on the Great Barrier Reef MPA website, are deceptive. Another researcher says the brochure "kills with the weight of innuendo."

Hoegh-Guldberg, for one, categorically denies overstating

any threat to the reef. He points out that researchers who have raised the alarm have had an uphill battle to force government and industry to take the threats seriously. But other coral experts believe the danger flag has been waved enough. The limited amount of money available for environmental protection needs to be divvied out on the basis of hard scientific facts, not emotional horse trading, they say. Scientific credibility is too precious to squander, especially when it comes to the Great Barrier Reef.

3

Global Warming Causes Coral Bleaching

Ove Hoegh-Guldberg

Marine biology professor Ove Hoegh-Guldberg, director of the Coral Reef Research Institute in Queensland, Australia, is a leading expert on the causes of coral reef stress. His report on the impact of global warming on coral bleaching helped persuade U.S. policy makers to set up the U.S. Coral Reef Initiative.

According to a report by marine biologist Ove Hoegh-Guldberg, a leading expert on coral bleaching, rising ocean temperatures as a result of global warming coincide with increases in coral bleaching. If nothing is done to stop global warming, he predicts coral bleaching will destroy coral reefs worldwide. Coral bleaching results when the microscopic plants that give coral its color are expelled by stress caused by rising ocean temperatures. Without these tiny plants, the coral turns white and dies. Many people depend on the coral reefs for food and the revenue reefs generate. Since greenhouse gases from the burning of fossil fuels are responsible for global warming, to protect threatened reefs, people must shift from using fossil fuels to using renewable energy resources.

If global warming is not stopped, coral bleaching is set to steadily increase in frequency and intensity all over the world until it occurs annually by 2030–2070.

This would devastate coral reefs globally to such an extent that they could be nonexistent in most areas of the world by 2100. Current estimates suggest that reefs could take hundreds of years to recover. The loss of these fragile ecosystems would cost hundreds of billions of dollars in lost revenue from tourism and fishing industries, as well as damage to coastal regions that are currently protected by the coral reefs that line most tropical coastlines.

> *// Current estimates suggest that reefs could take hundreds of years to recover. //*

[A] study, conducted by Professor Ove Hoegh-Guldberg, one of the world's leading experts in coral bleaching, uses the leading climate projection models from the Max Planck Institute in Germany and Australia's Commonwealth Scientific and Industrial Research Organisation (CSIRO)—two of the models used by the United Nation's Intergovernmental Panel on Climate Change to assess future climate change. By putting advanced climate and coral science together, he has been able to calculate time lines showing the fate of coral reefs if we continue to increase greenhouse gases in the atmosphere. The pattern of coral bleaching is consistent between all oceans. Coral bleaching will increase in frequency and intensity and is projected to devastate reef systems by early next century.

A bleak picture

Over the last few decades, coral reefs, renowned for their stunning beauty, extraordinary biodiversity, and high productivity have been under increasingly severe duress due to rising ocean temperatures. Throughout the world's oceans, from the Florida Keys to the Great Barrier Reef to the Indian Ocean, scientists have been witnessing unprecedented coral bleaching caused by rising ocean temperatures. Dr. Ove Hoegh-Guldberg's ground breaking scientific study uses the leading climate projection models to look at what is in store for the coral reefs if greenhouse gas emissions continue unabated. His findings, shown in this report, paint a bleak picture—ocean temperatures will continue escalating, causing massive coral bleaching events to increase in frequency and intensity. As early as 2030, the severe coral bleaching events that shocked the world's scientific and oceanic community in 1998, could become an annual occurrence. The report concludes, if the 'business as usual' scenario for our use of fossil fuels continues, our children may never be able to see coral reefs—by 2100 coral reefs will be nonexistent in many areas of the world. The loss of coral reefs would have devastating consequences, as they provide large sources of income for the tourism and fishing industries, ingredients for new drugs, and coastal protection from extreme weather events.

> *As early as 2030, the severe coral bleaching events that shocked the world's scientific and oceanic community in 1998, could become an annual occurrence.*

Thousand year old corals that have weathered well and withstood geological changes in the past, are suddenly dying. Prior to 1979, there is no scientific record of massive reef bleaching. Furthermore, there is no term for coral bleaching in the native language of societies that have lived with coral reefs for thousands of years. In short, mass coral bleaching is clearly a new phenomenon in all parts of the world.

The impact of coral reef destruction

The economic impact of these changes could run into trillions of dollars and would affect hundreds of millions of people worldwide. Globally, many people depend in part or wholly on coral reefs for their livelihood, and around half a billion people live within 60 miles of coral reef ecosystems. Tourism alone creates billions of dollars for countries associated with coral reefs—$1.6 billion generated annually by Floridean reefs; approximately $8.9 billion by Caribbean reefs and beach tourism; and $1.5 billion by Australia's Great Barrier Reef. The fisheries associated with coral reefs also generate significant wealth for countries with coral reef coastlines. Fisheries in coral reef areas also have importance beyond the mere generation of monetary wealth and are an essential source of protein for many millions of the world's poorer societies. For example, 25% of the fish catch in developing countries is provided from coral reef associated fisheries.

Tourism is the fastest growing economic sector associated

with coral reefs and is set to double in the very near future. One hundred million tourists visit the Caribbean each year. According to the U.S. State Department, SCUBA diving in the Caribbean alone is projected to generate $1.2 billion by the year 2005.

Coral bleaching is a condition that can seriously damage or kill entire reef systems. Corals contain microscopic plants called zooxanthellae, which vibrantly color their tissues and provide them with food via photosynthesis—the same process that plants use to manufacture food from sunlight. Without these tiny plants, corals cannot survive or lay down the huge amounts of limestone they produce for their skeletons. When corals become stressed, as from rising ocean temperatures, they expel the zooxanthellae and turn white or "bleach." If zooxanthellae do not return to the coral's tissue, the coral will die.

Because of the increasing intensity and geographic scale of recent bleaching events, mass bleaching is considered by most reef scientists to be a serious challenge to the health and prosperity of the world's coral reefs. The worst coral bleaching ever recorded took place in 1998. Every reef system in the world's tropical oceans was affected. In some places, such as the Indian Ocean, entire reef systems died.

The causes of coral bleaching

Tropical sea temperatures have increased by almost 1.8 degrees Fahrenheit (1 degree Celsius) over the past 100 years and are currently increasing at the rate of 1.8–3.6 degrees Fahrenheit (1–2° C) per century. Current evidence indicates that coral reefs can not adapt to this accelerated rate of warming. Increasing levels of greenhouse pollution from the burning of coal, oil and gas is increasing global temperatures to record levels. This report concludes that warmer ocean temperatures are the primary cause of the rise in intensity, frequency and extent of coral bleaching.

Over the last three decades we have experienced record temperatures, accompained by severe and lengthy El Niño's.[1] Since 1979 there have been six major episodes of worldwide massive coral bleaching—these episodes coincide with periods

---

1. El Niño is a warming of the ocean surface off the western coast of South America that occurs every four to twelve years when upwelling of cold, nutrient-rich water does not occur. It causes die-offs of plankton and fish and affects Pacific jet stream winds, altering storm tracks and creating unusual weather patterns in various parts of the world.

of warmer water temperature. Furthermore, there is compelling evidence that coral bleaching has not occurred with anywhere near this frequency prior to 1979. Corals are highly sensitive and can only live in water between 64–86 degrees Fahrenheit. Most bleaching events are explained by a 1.8 degree Fahrenheit (1 degree C) increase in temperature above the usual summer maximum water temperature. Global warming conditions are pushing corals past their thermal thresholds.

If we do not take urgent action to stop global warming, the next generation of children may not grow up to see beautiful, healthy coral reefs or many of the fish that populate them. The findings of this report show that due to increased sea temperatures from continued global warming, bleaching events will steadily increase in frequency and intensity. Within the next 30 years severe bleaching events are projected to occur every year in most tropical oceans.

In 1998, coral reefs were affected in 30 large-scale incidents worldwide, including the United States, Puerto Rico, Jamaica, the Bahamas, Australia, China, Japan, Panama, Thailand, Malaysia, the Philippines, India, Indonesia, Kenya, the Red Sea, and Okinawa. Events as severe as the 1998 event are projected to become an annual event by around the year 2020.

Globally, some regions will experience the effects of climate change on their reefs sooner than other areas. Caribbean and Southeast Asian coral reefs are projected to bleach every year by 2020. Central Pacific reefs are projected to experience bleaching every year by 2040. . . .

> *The worst coral bleaching ever recorded took place in 1998.*

Over the last few decades, corals have not shown any sign that they are able to adapt fast enough to keep pace with the present rapid changes in ocean temperature. Arguments that corals will adjust to predicted patterns of temperature change are unsubstantiated. Most evidence shows that bleaching events are an indicator that we are pushing corals past their thermal threshold, and their genetic ability to acclimate. If corals can adapt such changes are expected to take hundreds of years, suggesting that the quality of the world's reefs will decline at rates far faster than originally expected. This has enormous implications for the health and wealth of tropical and subtropical societies.

The additional threats to coral reefs

In addition to current and predicted rates of increase in sea surface temperature, coral reefs are also directly threatened by changes in atmospheric carbon dioxide and by rising sea levels. Current estimates show that atmospheric carbon dioxide levels expected around the middle of next century will inhibit the ability of corals to lay down their limestone skeletons by up to 30%. Because corals have to sustain high rates of skeletal construction to survive, this additional problem (together with coral bleaching) is expected to hasten the loss of coral reefs worldwide.

> **//** *Most evidence shows that bleaching events are an indicator that we are pushing corals past their thermal threshold, and their genetic ability to acclimate.* **//**

These changes, combined with the increasing stress on reefs from human-related activities, greenhouse gas pollution, over-exploitation of marine species, mining and oil drilling, and increased sedimentation, suggest that coral reefs may be dysfunctional within our lifetimes. Coral bleaching is vying to be the single largest casualty of "business-as-usual" greenhouse policies.

Although coral can recover from bleaching events, long-term or frequent bleaching may severely weaken the corals leaving them more vulnerable to disease, damage or death. In the Florida Keys, where scientists have set up 160 monitory stations, there has been a 400% increase in diseases from 1996 to the first part of 1999. In many cases large tracks of coral are dying. The report also concludes that higher temperatures reduce reproductive and growing capacities.

A need to save the reefs

This report expands on the mounting evidence that global warming is taking its toll on marine ecosystems. Dr. Ove Hoegh-Guldberg's findings along with the recent U.S. State Department report, Coral Bleaching, Coral Mortality, and Global Climate Change (released March 5, 1999), provide conclusive evidence that the future health of coral reefs are seriously jeopardized by continued global warming. While the Clinton Administration issued an Executive Order on the protection of coral reefs in June 1998, creating a U.S. Coral Reef Task Force that is charged with promoting conservation and sustainability of our rapidly dying coral reefs, very little has been done to tackle the root of the problem made clear in this report—rapidly rising greenhouse gas pollution from the burning of fossil fuels. If we are to avoid the loss of the world's coral reefs and critical marine ecosystems, the United States must prioritize and accelerate the transition away from our fossil fuel–based energy economy and begin to put in place the renewable energy solutions that are already available. Taxpayer dollars must be shifted away from subsidizing fossil fuel energy sources that are causing global warming and redirected to the development of clean, renewable energy solutions.

4

Global Warming Does Not Cause Coral Bleaching

Sallie Baliunas and Willie Soon

Sallie Baliunas is an astrophysicist at the Harvard-Smithsonian Center for Astrophysics in Cambridge, Massachusetts, deputy director of Mount Wilson Observatory, and cohost of TechCentralStation.com, a Web site that promotes technology and free trade. Willie Soon, a physicist at the Harvard-Smithsonian Center for Astrophysics and an astronomer at Mount Wilson Observatory, is science director at TechCentralStation.com.

Claims that global warming causes coral bleaching are exaggerated. Coral samples show that 250 years ago, before industrial emissions entered the atmosphere, temperatures in the South Pacific were two Celsius degrees higher than those measured today, yet coral reefs still flourished. In 1995, rising water temperatures were blamed for a mass bleaching of the western Atlantic and Caribbean reefs. By 1996, however, almost all the corals had recovered, proving that global warming itself does not destroy coral reefs. Coral reefs are not indestructible, but more attention should be paid to human activities that are proven to cause destruction instead of wasting billions of dollars on scientifically unjustified and unworkable emissions programs designed to reduce coral bleaching.

The issue is coral reefs, the sea's rainforests so vital for fisheries, coastal protection and, because of their great beauty,

Sallie Baliunas and Willie Soon, "Beware Reef-er Madness at Marrakech Climate Conference," *Tech Central Station*, October 29, 2001. Copyright © 2001 by *Tech Central Station*. Reproduced by permission.

tourism. And The United Nations Environmental Programme [UNEP] announced [in 2001] the most detailed assessment of reefs' health yet.

The new UNEP Atlas claims 58% of the world's coral reefs are threatened by human activities like dynamite fishing, local pollution and global warming. According to the Australian Institute of Marine Science, which provided much of the groundwork for the UNEP report, 27% of the world's coral reefs have been lost, "with the largest single cause being the massive climate-related coral bleaching event of 1998."

But a close examination of the basis for blaming human-made global warming for the loss of coral reefs—and posing a huge threat to them in the future—lacks substance. And at a practical level, the overly heavy focus on human-induced warming as the source of reef degradation may damage other worthy efforts to coral reefs.

Coral reefs are not disappearing

The UNEP story begins with some pessimistic puffery claiming coral reefs occupy a "smaller area of the planet than previously assumed." All that has really happened, though, is welcome progress in reducing ignorance about the scope of reefs.

UNEP's latest assessment claims 284,300 square kilometers of reefs exist worldwide, or 110,000 square miles. Now, several measures of the size of coral reefs around the globe have been made, and they've yielded a wide range of results—from 100,000 square kilometers to nearly 4,000,000 square kilometres, depending on how reefs are defined. Taking the high-end estimate, it could appear that reefs are disappearing.

> *The overly heavy focus on human-induced warming as the source of reef degradation may damage other worthy efforts to protect coral reefs.*

But UNEP had a decent baseline set [in 1997], when Mark Spalding, the co-leader of the UNEP's global assessment effort, estimated the area for coral reefs as 255,000 square kilometers. So on that basis, coral reefs now occupy 29,000 square kilometers more area than previously thought. So UNEP's latest claim—that reefs occupy a smaller area of the planet—is contradicted by its own estimates.

Ocean temperatures are not rising

Far more serious, though, are the faulty connections attempting to tie "bleaching"—or whitening—of coral reefs with human-induced global warming by the burning of fossil fuels.

The idea posits that gradual human-made warming of the air either warms the water in tropical regions above levels at which coral polyps—algae that support the reefs' biosystems—can survive. Australia's Marine Institute, for example, claimed the Pacific bleaching it recorded was "caused by the combination of extremely calm conditions during the 1997–98 El Niño-La Niña events,[1] coupled with a steadily rising baseline of sea surface temperatures in the tropics," which it then parenthetically added was "increasingly attributed to greenhouse warming."

There are problems, though, in such claims.

> *The increase in human-made greenhouse gases has not caused coral bleaching.*

First, there has been no systematic increase in the severity in El Niño events over the last 100 years, according to the record shown by the U.N. Intergovernmental Panel on Climate Change. So greenhouse gas increases do not raise El Niño intensity. That means that the increase in human-made greenhouse gases has not caused coral bleaching.

The best estimate from instrumental measurements shows only a very modest increase—a few tenths of a degree Celsius—in surface ocean temperature of the southern hemisphere in recent decades. But as Mark A. Cane and Michael Evans noted in

---

1. El Niño is a warming of the ocean surface off the western coast of South America that occurs every four to twelve years when upwelling of cold, nutrient-rich water does not occur. It causes die-offs of plankton and fish and affects Pacific jet stream winds, altering storm tracks and creating unusual weather patterns in various parts of the world. La Niña is the opposite of El Niño; a major cooling occurs in the equatorial waters in the Pacific Ocean that is characterized by shifts in "normal" weather patterns.

an editorial in [the November 2000 issue of] *Science*, instrumental data only scantily cover the South Pacific and go back at most a little over a century. That's a narrow window in which to measure natural changes that affect the estimate of any man-made trend.

> *Suggestions that human-caused global warming [has] devastated these [coral reef] systems have not panned out.*

And the temperature trends for rising ocean surface water temperatures, like those for air, are not increasing linearly. The so-called Great Pacific Climate Shift of 1976–77 has influenced them. First instrumentally observed only since 1900, that shift in the North Pacific—also called the Pacific Decadal Oscillation—recurs in patterns that can last two or three decades. Braddock K. Linsley, Gerard M. Wellington and Daniel P. Schrag were able to establish through coral samples near the island of Rarotonga a similar climate record for the South Pacific dating back 271 years. Their report, in the same edition of *Science* as the Cane and Evans editorial, showed South Pacific temperatures 250 years ago that were 2 degrees celsius higher than those measured today.

The impact of human-induced global warming

Such markedly higher water temperatures prior to the onset of the industrial age, and the fact that coral communities survived, undercut the notion that human-induced global warming is a real cause of concern for coral reefs. Coral blooms may be far more resilient than proponents of human-caused global warming ideas believe.

In 1995, monitoring teams in the Western Atlantic and Caribbean reported abnormally high levels of coral bleaching, with overall bleaching of reefs reaching 14% and one major reef—Lindsay Reef—found with 42% of its surface area bleached. The bleaching was blamed on rising water temperatures. By July 1996, though, according to a study by Thomas A. McGrath and Garriet W. Smith reported in *Revista de Biologia Tropical*, almost all the corals had recovered.

It isn't that coral reefs are indestructible. They can be and have been damaged. But coral reefs have declined and revived from short-term temperature fluctuations, and they have survived and adapted to some longer episodes as well. Suggestions that human-caused global warming [has] devastated these systems have not panned out.

The factors that harm coral reefs

However, real human-caused local problems that affect coral reefs demand attention.

Coral reefs suffer from overfishing, use of chemicals and explosives to bring fish to the surface, and contamination from agricultural discharge. As Jerome Jackson and 18 other scientists reported in the July 27 [2001] issue of *Science*, overfishing is likely the underlying cause of most coral reef degradation. Overfishing kills key sea animals that clean reef waters and seabeds, while also eliminating important predators that keep in check starfish that feed on coral polyps.

The answer to these problems won't be found by curtailing emissions of carbon dioxide, which is as necessary to life in the seas as it is on land. Rather, just the opposite of global action—local action—is vital to reef health. The United States protects the Dry Tortugas 70 miles off of Key West. Forty countries, though, accounting for a substantial area of the world's coral reefs, have no marine protected areas for their coral reef system.

To encourage such action in Latin America and the Caribbean, the House [in October 2001] passed a measure sponsored by Rep. Mark Kirk of Illinois to provide debt relief credit for money spent preserving coral reefs.

Workable solutions are needed

This direct approach to preservation is far preferable to wasting hundreds of billions on unworkable solutions designed to lower carbon dioxide emissions.

A sharp cutback in fossil fuel use, as proponents of the Kyoto protocol desire, would have little effect on the temperature of the oceans—either now or in the future. Implementation would cut temperature forecast less than 0.1 degrees Celsius by 2050, and sea temperatures even less.

But while doing nothing to help save reefs, the Kyoto Protocol will severely cost developed nations in dramatically reduced economic growth—$300 billion a year for the United States alone. Less economic growth could quickly lead to less money going into reef protection.

Thus, those who push uneconomic and scientifically unjustified curbs on greenhouse gas emissions may end up hurting the ocean environment far more than preserving and protecting it.

5

Coral Reefs Face Many Natural and Human Threats

Brian J. English

Brian J. English, a certified diver, works with Coastal Resource Assessment Training, a training program that teaches divers how to gather socioeconomic and environmental data related to coastal resource management.

Both natural and human threats contribute to coral reef degradation. Natural threats include coral predators such as the crown-of-thorns starfish that disrupt the balance of the reef ecosystem. Climate change, storms, and volcanoes can also disrupt the complex coral ecosystem. However, studies show that human threats pose the greatest danger to the reefs. Sediment from coastal construction, for example, covers corals that need light to survive. Some researchers claim that human behavior also contributed to what are often seen as natural threats. When locals and tourists collect too many reef shells, for example, they kill predators of the crown-of-thorns starfish, thus providing an explanation for starfish overpopulation.

Although corals evolved more than 450 million years ago and most coral reefs now are between 5,000 and 10,000 years old, there is still a growing international concern about the widespread global degradation of coral reefs and their related ecosystems. Overuse and abuse of coral reefs are increasing exponentially because the human population is increasing exponentially. Although some natural phenomena such as earthquakes, typhoons, climate changes, coral eating predators and plagues may cause threats to marine ecosystems, human activity accounts for the majority of degradation to coral reefs. Siltation, population, poor coastal planning and inappropriate fishing techniques are some of the ways that humans threaten marine estuaries and ecosystems. This paper will first explain the severity of various natural and human factors that threaten coral communities, and then suggest plausible action to countervail those threats.

> *Increases in the population of a coral predator can have a devastating impact on the coral colony.*

The first section of the paper will discuss natural threats to corals beginning with immediate predators and diseases living in marine environments and ending with larger scale natural threats that may result from changes in the environment. The second section of the paper will address the human threat to coral reefs beginning with direct degradation of reefs and ending with causal analysis of possible indirect threat to marine coastal environments.

The threat of coral diseases

Corals are living animals so it logically follows that they are part of the food chain. In a healthy environment corals can be expected to grow and multiply in spite of the presence of predators. Equilibrium relationships between prey and predator may continue for a number of years and suddenly be interrupted by a population explosion. Increases in the population of a coral predator can have a devastating impact on the coral colony. One such predator that periodically reaches plague numbers is the crown-of-thorns starfish. Numbers of these coral digesting starfish can reach into the hundreds of thousands, yet there is only speculation as to what may cause the outbreaks. The normal-event hypothesis suggests that environmental factors such as temperature, salinity and availability of food are causal variables in outbreaks. There is speculation that in years when conditions are favorable due to natural fluctuation in atmospheric and bio-spheric conditions, more planktotrophic larvae will survive to settle on reefs setting the state for a population explosion. The second section of this paper will discuss two anthoropogenic feedback scenarios that may account for the outbreaks.

> **"** *Red tide is often documented as a threat to coral communities.* **"**

Although outbreaks of coral eating predators can kill off large portions of a colony, it is possible the colony will recover in less than 15 years. [M.W.] Colgan (1987) did a longitudinal study at Tanguisson Reef in Guam, which suffered an outbreak of coral eating starfish in the late 1960s. Colgan found that the reef had almost fully recovered within 12 years. However, Colgan reasons that since, in this case, the starfish did not destroy the structural integrity of the reef, the recovery was quicker than had been predicted. [R.] Endean and [A.M.] Cameron (1990) give several accounts of, and provide a detailed discussion on outbreaks of coral eating starfish.

The coral predators

Corals are prey to other corallivores like parrotfish and urchins, but perhaps the deadliest enemies are the smallest. Bacterial damage to corals is often associated with "coral bleaching" which is a condition that causes corals to lose their coloring. Since corals get their color from the zooxanthellae algae that symbiotically live inside the coral, disruption to the symbiotic relationship can result in a bleaching effect. [L.L.] Richardson (1998) has documented evidence of the spread of a deadly bacterium from the coastal Florida waters through parts of the Caribbean. Despite identifying the disease, the researcher and her team were unable to determine the origin of the disease or the reasons for its rapid spreading. Similar bacterial attacks have been documented from the Arabian Gulf to the Indian Ocean. The various strands of this disease are referred to as Black Band, White Band and Yellow Band.

Red tide is often documented as a threat to coral communities. Red tide are just one type of algae that can negatively impact coral growth and reproduction. Algae blooms can block sunlight which both corals and their symbiotic partners, zooxanthallae (the "good algae") need to survive. Algae blooms also reduce oxygen levels in the water and some species release toxins that can also harm corals and zooxanthellae. There is still speculation on what causes algae blooms, but one explanation is similar to that for starfish population explosions. When conditions are optimal there are algae blooms. Both natural and anthropogenic eutrophication are probable variables in producing optimal conditions for algae blooms.

The natural environmental threats to coral

Since coral communities are an intricate part of coastal environments they are subject to the awesome forces of nature. [R.W.] Grigg and [S.J.] Dollar (1990) site a number of studies that document major disturbances and mortality of coral communities caused by low temperatures, storms, major El Niño[1] seasonal changes, low tides, and volcanic eruptions earthquakes.

Although coral bleaching can be caused by the presence of parasitic bacteria feeding on the zooxanthellae algae living in the coral pulp, [A.] Kushmaro [Y. Loyola, M. Fine, and E. Rosenberg] (1996) acknowledge that disruptions to the symbiotic relationship with zooxanthellae could also result from increased seawater temperature, ultraviolet radiation and climate change. [R.D.] Gates (1990) studied the effects of seawater on corals in Jamaica. Gates found much of the bleaching effects to be seasonal and not always lethal to the coral. If minor seasonal fluctuations in temperature can cause sublethal coral bleaching, does more severe seawater temperature change cause lethal bleaching?

Coral reefs may also be damaged by storms and hurricanes. Although the effect is usually minimal, severe storms may do visible damage to reef systems. [S.M.] Blair, [T.L.] McIntosh and [B.J.] Mostkoff (1994) documented the effects of hurricane Andrew on soft and hard coral systems in southern Florida. They concluded that the hurricane affected the benthic cover of algal and soft

---

1. El Niño is a warming of the ocean surface off the western coast of South America that occurs every four to twelve years when upwelling of cold, nutrient-rich water does not occur. It causes die-offs of plankton and fish and affects Pacific jet stream winds, altering storm tracks and creating unusual weather patterns in various parts of the world.

coral communities were heavily impacted, whereas the benthic cover of hard corals was slightly to moderately impacted.

Research in Australia and throughout the Pacific describes how the El Niño–Southern oscillation event is responsible for aperiodic influences on corals. The El Niño phenomenon causes changes in surface temperature, wind fields and rainfall. Increased rainfall may be the strongest of these three variables because it leads to increased river flow and run off. Still, Lough did not find any major damage or change in the structure or health of the corals in the Great Barrier Reef due to the El Niño phenomenon, but he acknowledges the need to consider high variability in the physical environment when examining changes in reef processes due to global change or human degradation.

> *Severe storms may do visible damage to reef systems.*

Because corals need salt water to live, low tides that expose surface coral can result in bleaching and death of near surface reef corals. Similarly, in regions where there are heavy seasonal rains, fresh water runoff from mountains and rivers can reduce the salinity of the water affecting the health of corals. Certainly, this type of seasonal stress to corals is not as detrimental as more catastrophic occurrences such as earthquakes and volcanoes that destroy the structural integrity of reefs over vast areas. In the long term, the impact that naturally occurring periodic changes in climate and ecosystems have on corals is dependent on the magnitude and return period. Grigg and Dollar analyzed species composition and community structure of coral reefs in the Hawaiian archipelago to develop a theoretical model of succession that suggests "differences between reef communities in comparable habitats off different islands are due largely to differences in successional age." If the recovery time is less than the return period of severe disturbances, then reefs are usually high cover, dominated by one or only a few species, and have low diversity. Conversely, reef systems that have frequent disturbances (i.e., seasonal storms, high waves, or periodic low tides) are characterized as having "low cover, high diversity, high equitability."

Corals have a natural ability to recover from natural "disturbances"; however, the human disturbances to coral communities can impact marine environments more severely. According to the National Oceanic and Atmospheric Administration (NOAA):

> The most serious anthropogenic stresses include: sedimentation caused by poor land-use practices; pollution and over-nutrification from domestic, agricultural, and industrial waste; physical alteration of coral reefs during coastal construction projects; destructive fishing practices such as poison and blast fishing; ship groundings; and coastal tourism, which brings millions of eager divers and snorkellers to coral-rich areas of the world each year.

These variables and their causal links to coral degradation will be discussed in this section.

According to Grigg and Dollar (1990) sedimentation poses the most common and the most serious anthropogenic threat to corals. Sedimentation is often linked to expanding human populations. More people translates into more buildings. Construction of buildings may involve products made from corals such as cement or limestone. Coral mining not only destroys the corals being mined, but also disturbs the greater marine eco-system by clouding the water with sediment and smothering corals. Construction near the shore also creates muddy estuaries and lagoons. Inland, too, certain practices can add to the increase in sedimentation. Clear-cut logging, deforestation, inappropriate farming methods, mining for ore and removing vegetation from banks can greatly increase the amount of river run-off.

> *Because corals need salt water to live, low tides that expose surface coral can result in bleaching and death of near surface reef corals.*

Corals are able to withstand some levels of sedimentation because in the natural environment sediment particles are suspended in seawater. Griggs and Dollar (1990) assert that most coral species can withstand only a low level of sediment supply to the living surface. Corals have a natural sediment-rejection capacity. "Many species have the ability to remove sediment from their tissues by distension of the coenosarc with water, or by ciliary action which can nullify lethal effects of sedimentation." Although corals can naturally "clean" some of the sediments from their system, corals are unable to deal with major sedimentation caused by either cataclysmic natural disaster or by massive anthropogenic disturbances.

> *Some of the diseases that attack corals might also have connections to human behavior.*

Much needs to be done to circumvent the impact that human-origin sedimentation has on corals. One idea includes sewage abatement processes. If sewer outfalls are placed at depths below reef growth, there may be less effect on the reef. Still, the best way to avoid destroying coral reefs may be to educate people on how to reduce sedimentation in marine ecosystems.

Finding connections to human behavior

As mentioned earlier, the crown-of-thorns starfish has periodic outbreaks that increase its predacious effect on corals. Although there is little current evidence to support the role of humans in these outbreaks, [D.E.] McAllister and [A.] Ansula (1993) suggest the elimination of crown-of-thorns' natural enemies through over-collecting of their shells may be one factor. With fewer natural enemies, the equilibrium is upset and the starfish are able to multiply until the reduction of their own food supplies force declines in population. They also describe the plausibility that over-fertilizing is a causal factor in increasing numbers of these starfish, "Fertilizers from farms, sewage or other sources wash on to coral reefs and cause blooms of tiny plants called phytoplankton. The survival of the larvae, . . . is better on this rich source of food, and more grow up to be an adult."

Some of the diseases that attack corals might also have connections to human behavior. Richardson (1998) claims the Black Band disease that destroys coral tissue originates from a group of algae that secrete toxic sulfides into the marine environment. C.R. Wilkinson suggests anthropogenic factors for the increases of algae. Pollution from oil and petrochemical industries and other human threats to the marine environment have decreased fish populations and provided conditions conducive to algae blooms. [E.] Hierta (1994) claims, "Excessive nutrients from sewage and agricultural runoff spur algae blooms, such as red or brown tides, that can smother coral. Turbidity from sediment runoff blocks any sunlight needed for growth."

The primary threat

Although there are many natural threats to marine ecosystems, corals have evolved into animals that are able to recover from environmental and predatory threats. Many of the established coral reefs in the world today have been thriving and surviving for thousands of years. Despite the natural ability to persist, many coral reef ecosystems are in poor health. The recent major declines in coral reef health can be traced to anthropogenic origins. Inappropriate fishing practices and development related causes are destroying reefs at alarming rates. Humans are currently a major threat to coral.

> *Ironically, it may be humans and human technology [that] rescues ailing coral reefs.*

Ironically, it may be humans and human technology [that] rescues ailing coral reefs. Grigg and Dollar optimistically claim "the technology to mitigate impacts of many sources of anthropogenic stress are presently available." They give examples of sewage abatement, deep-water disposal, containment booms and adsorbents (for oil spills).

Coral reef management at the local level may offer the best answer to anthropogenic stress. Community-based environment education programs are becoming popular in many areas where coral reefs have been damaged. As a form of non-formal education these programs aim to help local residents of coastal communities learn how maintain a sustainable relationship with the marine environment.

One impressive example of coral reef management is in the Philippines. By the mid-1980s, Apo Reef was almost totally destroyed by villagers' inappropriate fishing practices. The use of dynamite, cyanide and destructive nets to eke out a living from the failing reef nearly destroyed the island community's liveli-hood. Apo Reef has made a dramatic comeback in the last decade and a half due to proactive reef management by the lo-cal community and experts from Silliman University in Du-maguete. The villagers have learned sustainable practices that are essential to maintaining healthy reefs. [D.] Hinrichsen comments on the hope that the Apo Reef case provides for community-based coral reef management programs:

> Apo demonstrates that it is not too late to protect these wonderfully diverse underwater ecosystems and to preserve their productivity for the people who depend on them. The model that Apo sets of-fers encouragement to the coral-reef nations that recently launched a new international protection plan, culminating in the designation of 1997 as the International Year of the Coral Reef.

This paper only gives a general overview of the threats to coral reefs. Many of the anthropogenic threats have roots in the political, economic and social institutions of society. To be-gin to seek solutions to the human causes of coral reef degra-dation, it is necessary that scientists and researchers engage in interdisciplinary efforts sharing their knowledge and resources.

6

Cyanide Fishing Threatens Coral Reefs

Charles Victor Barbor and Vaughan R. Pratt

Charles Victor Barbor is Southeast Asia field projects coordinator in the Biological Resources Program of the World Resources Institute (WRI) in Washington, D.C. Vaughan R. Pratt is president of the International Marinelife Alliance in Pasig City, the Philippines.

The practice of squirting cyanide on coral reefs to stun and capture live fish is destroying coral reefs. Cyanide kills live coral and the reef organisms that sustain it. Cyanide fishing is also detrimental to the health of the exploited divers, who spend too much time under water using dangerous equipment. Cyanide fishing has spread worldwide because of the demand for live food fish in Asian countries and for aquarium fish. Because the practice is so lucrative for those who import and export live fish, governments are reluctant to develop or enforce laws that protect coral reefs from the deadly poison. Communities need to educate their people about the dangers to themselves and the coral reefs they look to for their livelihood.

Aboard the *Morning Sun* in the grey Hong Kong dawn just before Christmas 1997, a stocky Chinese stevedore stood waist-deep in a tank with dozens of furiously thrashing napoleon wrasse, one of the most spectacular of Asia's coral reef fishes. One by one, he wrestled the fish, some weighing nearly 30 kg. into a scoop net and into the hands of his co-workers on

Charles Victor Barbor and Vaughan R. Pratt, "Poison and Profits: Cyanide Fishing in the Indo-Pacific," *Environment*, October 1998. Copyright © 1998 by the Helen Dwight Reid Educational Foundation. Reproduced by permission of the Helen Dwight Reid Educational Foundation. Published by Heldref Publications, 1319 18th St. NW, Washington, DC 20036-1802.

the dock above. Weighed and sold right on the dock for as much as $90 per kilogram, the fish were hustled off in minutes into waiting trucks equipped with their own holding tanks. By evening, some of them would be sold to elite Hong Kong diners willing to pay up to $180 per kilogram—and up to $225 per plate for the wrasse's lips, the most prized of reef fish delicacies.

> **❝** *Since the 1960s, more than a million kilograms of cyanide have been squirted onto coral reefs in the Philippines.* **❞**

By the time the *Morning Sun* had unloaded, some 20 tons of live reef fish—8 tons of napoleon wrasse and 12 tons of assorted grouper species—were on their way to the districts where diners pick their fish from tanks at specialized shops for cooking in adjacent restaurants. The *Morning Sun*'s catch, which came from Indonesian waters, was just a drop in the bucket, however: Some 20,000 tons of live reef food fish were imported into Hong Kong in 1997. The scene that December morning was just one link in a chain of poison and profits that is bringing destruction to some of the planet's most pristine and biologically diverse coral reefs: The fish on the *Morning Sun* were almost certainly captured by applying hundreds of kilograms of cyanide, the most lethal broad-spectrum poison known to science, across vast areas of Indonesia's coral reefs.

A growing international trade

In other cultures, live reef fish are prized more for their ornamental than their culinary value, and the international trade in aquarium fish—85 percent of which are captured in the Indo-Pacific—is driven by demand in Europe and North America. The impact is the same, however, because cyanide is also the preferred method for capturing such fish. Whether it is about to be steamed with ginger sauce in a Hong Kong restaurant or it is swimming in a tank at a dentist's office in California, any live reef fish from the Indo-Pacific region was very likely captured with some form of cyanide.

Since the 1960s, more than a million kilograms of cyanide have been squirted onto coral reefs in the Philippines to stun and capture ornamental aquarium fish destined for the pet shops and aquariums of Europe and North America. More recently, the growing demand for live reef fish as food in Hong Kong and other major Asian cities has vastly increased the incidence of the practice. Strong demand has spread cyanide fishing throughout Indonesia and into such neighboring countries as Papua New Guinea and Malaysia. In [1998], officials in countries as far-flung as Eritrea, the Marshall Islands, the Solomon Islands, and Vietnam have voiced suspicions that their fast-growing live fish export industries are also using cyanide.

> *The fishermen have to use crowbars to pry coral heads apart and retrieve the stunned fish.*

Cyanide fishing itself is fairly simple: Fishermen first crush cyanide pellets into makeshift squirt bottles filled with seawater. Then they dive down to coral formations and squirt the cyanide solution into the crevices where fish hide. The cyanide stuns the fish, making them easier to capture. In some cases, however, the fishermen have to use crowbars to pry coral heads apart and retrieve the stunned fish.

Poison for profit

Cyanide fishing can be a very lucrative business, at least for the vessel and holding-tank operators, exporters, and importers involved in the trade. Military, police, and other officials are also paid well for looking the other way. The divers, by contrast, are usually exploited by those who organize and supply the fishing operations.

This type of fishing exacts a heavy toll, however, both from those engaged in it and from the environment. For divers, the most immediate health threat is not from cyanide but from the fact that they spend long hours at considerable depths (often 15–25 meters) breathing through tubes attached to air compressors. As a result of the length of time they spend submerged, divers often suffer from decompression sickness ("the bends") upon returning to the surface. Nor is the air they breathe underwater necessarily healthy: The compressors that supply it are often refitted paint compressors on which the intake and exhaust valves are close together, which causes the divers to breathe in large amounts of carbon monoxide. There have been no systematic studies of the effects of such practices on divers' health, however.

The unknown dangers

The risks of eating fish caught with cyanide are also unknown. It is likely, however, that fish sold live pose little risk to human health because of the relatively rapid rate at which (it is thought) fish metabolize and excrete cyanide. Not all fish that are caught with cyanide are exported alive, however: Those that die in the process are often consumed locally. (Cyanide is also sometimes added to the bait used to catch fish with a hook and line.) Dead fish, of course, do not metabolize the cyanide, which tends to accumulate in the internal organs, especially the liver. The risks of eating such fish have not been studied but may be significant (particularly in Asia where people eat—and sometimes prefer—the internal organs).

> *Cyanide fishing is . . . very destructive to the coral reef ecosystems in which it is practiced.*

Cyanide fishing is also very destructive to the coral reef ecosystems in which it is practiced. Large percentages of the fish that are captured live die in transit due to their poison-weakened state, meaning that many more fish have to be taken than are actually needed. In addition, cyanide kills coral and reef invertebrates along with many nontarget fish. The extent to which exposure to cyanide injures or kills the organisms that make up coral reefs themselves has not been studied extensively and thus is not really known. A field test in the Philippines in 1980 showed that two exposures to cyanide three months apart can completely kill the exposed reef area. Laboratory tests at the University of Guam in 1995 indicated that exposures as low as 1 part in 10 million could kill corals. Experiments at the Great Barrier Reef in 1995 suggested "a deleterious effect of cyanide fishing on corals in the immediate vicinity." The researcher who conducted these experiments noted, however, that it is difficult to estimate the level of exposure to cyanide from fishing. The initial exposure is likely to be high (i.e., parts per thousand), but it probably declines to low levels (parts per billion) within hours or even seconds, depending on currents.

In addition to these formal scientific findings, there is a good deal of anecdotal evidence about the effects of cyanide fishing on corals. Deleterious effects were first reported in the Philippines during the 1980s. A [1996] report [by M.V. Erdmann and L. Pet-Soede] from eastern Indonesia states that fishermen and divers "are adamant that the live fish business is responsible for empty reefs throughout the Philippines and Indonesia, and industry representatives give several examples of archipelagoes that are exhausted." [R.E. Johannes and M. Riepen] report that cyanide fishermen in those two countries "invariably asserted that cyanide causes extensive damage to corals." In addition, divers and dive-tour operators say that cyanide fishing has caused the "total destruction" of reefs—including the corals, other invertebrates, and fish. In short, there is ample evidence that cyanide kills corals, but questions remain about the necessary level of exposure, the effects of repeated exposure, and the relative susceptibility of different kinds of coral.

Growing awareness in the Indo-Pacific

Deadly in any marine environment, cyanide fishing is particularly tragic in the Indo-Pacific, which possesses some 70 percent of the planet's coral reefs and is the global center of biodiversity for corals, fish, mollusks, and reef invertebrates. Cyanide fishing also threatens the livelihood of poor coastal people in the region, where dependence on fish protein is very high and fishing provides millions with income.

> *A field test in the Philippines in 1980 showed that two exposures to cyanide three months apart can completely kill the exposed [coral] reef area.*

The Philippines, which is the birthplace of cyanide fishing, is also the only country with a program to eradicate the practice. Since the early 1990s, the Bureau of Fisheries and Aquatic Resources and the Philippine branch of the International

Marinelife Alliance (IMA), a nongovernmental organization, have been developing and implementing a broadly based Destructive Fishing Reform Program. Experience with this program . . . shows that cyanide fishing can be reduced through a combination of the right policies and laws; beefed-up enforcement efforts; enhanced public awareness; testing of live fish exports; training of cyanide fishermen in alternative techniques; and the development of sustainable, community-based resource management and livelihood programs that transform local fishermen into frontline marine stewards.

The live reef fish trade

The live reef fish trade in Southeast Asia has an estimated annual retail value of $1.2 billion (U.S. dollars), $1 billion of which consists of exports of food fish (mostly to Hong Kong) and $200 million of which consists of exports of aquarium fish to Europe and North America. Not all of these fish are caught with cyanide (Australia's live reef fishery, for example, is cyanide-free), but a very large percentage are. To understand the dynamics of this trade, it is necessary to be familiar with the various actors involved and the incentives that motivate their behavior.

First on the list are the cyanide fishermen themselves. The number of such fishermen operating in the Indo-Pacific region is not known. However, based on estimates for the Philippines (where there are about 4,000), the total number probably does not exceed 20,000. Thus, cyanide fishing is not a ubiquitous problem like slash-and-burn agriculture, which is practiced by millions of poor farmers. Nor is poverty the root cause of cyanide fishing, although many of those who engage in it are quite poor. On the contrary, cyanide fishermen are a fairly small and discrete group who are responding to very specific incentives: a new technology, a ready market for the product, lax government enforcement of anti-cyanide laws, and the lack of viable alternatives for making a living.

Next on the list are the exporters. The number of companies engaged in exporting live reef fish in the Indo-Pacific region is also unknown, but it appears to be expanding rapidly. In the early 1960s, for example, there were only three companies exporting aquarium fish from the Philippines and none exporting live food fish. By the 1990s, there were some 45 aquarium fish exporters in the country and 8 companies exporting live food fish. At least 10 companies have holding tanks for live food fish in Bali, Indonesia, a major transhipment point. Conservative estimates of the annual volume of Asian trade in live food fish range from 20,000 to 25,000 metric tons (mostly from Indonesia), though the real total may be far greater. Philippine government statistics show that as many as 6 million aquarium fish were exported from that country in 1996, and Indonesia is catching up quickly.

> *Consumers can play an important role in pressuring the aquarium-fish industry to reduce imports of fish caught with cyanide.*

Closely related to the exporters are the businesses that import live food and aquarium fish. These businesses, in fact, are in essentially the same position as exporters: Without pressure from the government to ensure that the fish they import were not caught with cyanide, they have little incentive to take action on the issue. As one large importer has argued, "We . . . importers do not participate in any catching of fish or its activities. We just finance the people by equipping them with boats and fishing gear. We just buy fish from them. The production side is left to them."

The last actors in the live reef fish trade are the consumers of these fish. Experience shows that consumers can play an important role in pressuring the aquarium-fish industry to reduce imports of fish caught with cyanide. Indeed, bad publicity and the ensuing consumer pressure in the United States have recently led to efforts to certify imported aquarium fish as having been caught using sustainable methods. Opposition to cyanide fishing is virtually nonexistent among the Chinese consumers of live food fish, however. As one Hong Kong observer has remarked, "being endangered actually seems to spur demand."

Putting an end to cyanide fishing

In the face of powerful economic pressures, is there any hope of curtailing cyanide fishing? The answer is "yes," provided the right approach is taken. Experience in the Philippines and, more recently, Indonesia suggests that an effective anti-cyanide strategy must combine three elements. First, the governments of the source countries must reform their policies and strengthen their institutions to effectively deal with the problem. Second, the governments of the importing countries must take steps that reinforce the measures taken by the source countries. Third, and most fundamentally, there must be strong partnerships with those on the front lines, that is, the fishing communities and fishermen in areas where cyanide fishing is practiced. . . .

Cyanide fishing is not the only threat to the coral reefs and other coastal ecosystems of the Indo-Pacific region. Others include the rapid conversion of coastal habitats such as mangrove swamps for aquaculture or the production of charcoal; overfishing due to excess fleet capacity stemming from government subsidies; dynamite fishing; haphazard tourism development; pollution by factories and mines, along with contamination by urban wastes, fertilizers, and pesticides; and sedimentation related to deforestation. But the training and community-organization strategies essential to stopping cyanide fishing should provide an important catalyst for communities to address these threats as well.

The difficulty of putting an end to cyanide fishing should not be underestimated. It is important to note, however, that people have long caught and sold live fish without using cyanide and that they still do in places such as Australia, the Caribbean, and Hawaii. Nothing is intrinsically wrong with a cyanide-free live fish trade as long as it is practiced sustainably and protects the coral reef ecosystems that provide habitat for the fish. But cyanide fishing is fast becoming a deadly tradition in many countries of the Indo-Pacific. The challenge is to swiftly eradicate that tradition and ensure that the greatest coral reefs on the planet survive into the 21st century.

7

African Dust May Threaten Coral Reefs

John C. Ryan

John C. Ryan writes on global sustainability for the World-watch Institute and has authored several books, including Seven Wonders: Everyday Things for a Healthier Planet.

Researchers have found a new explanation for the degradation of Caribbean coral reefs: Reef pathogens are being carried along with airborne dust from Africa. For years scientists have been unable to explain why Caribbean reefs suffered from severe disturbances such as bacterial damage and coral bleaching. Some researchers, however, believe that the bacteria killing the coral accompanies dust that is carried by the trade winds across the Atlantic Ocean from Africa. These scientists have compared periods of Caribbean coral reef decline with peak African dust events and have noted a correlation. The hypothesis is controversial, however, because proving a causal relationship is difficult. In addition, some believe that blaming African dust diverts attention and resources away from human causes and the management efforts that protect coral reefs from exploitation.

African dust is nothing new to the Caribbean. Residents have long suffered through the occasional sinus-clogging haze or risen some mornings to find their islands coated in a thin layer of fine red powder. Dust carried by trade winds across the Atlantic from Africa's Sahel occasionally reduces visibility and reddens skies from Miami to Caracas, sometimes even forcing airports to close. Pre-Columbian natives in the eastern Bahamas crafted pottery from windborne deposits of African clay;

agriculture in the Bahamas today depends largely on the red soils known as pineapple loam, composed of African dust deposited millennia ago.

Though mariners and researchers ever since Darwin have observed African particulates carried aloft hundreds of miles into the Atlantic, studies of atmospheric dust have focused mostly on its impacts on global heat budgets and carbon cycles. Only recently have researchers begun exploring the possibility that the hundreds of millions of tons of African aerosols landing annually in the Caribbean might have major, direct impacts on the region's marine ecosystems—and even on public health.

With all the other forces working to unravel the Caribbean's ecosystems—from global climate change to local water quality—some reef scientists and reef managers have seen the red dust as a red herring. But an increasing body of evidence, along with increasing loads of airborne pathogens and nutrients, is making it harder to ignore these transatlantic inputs to the troubled marine ecosystems of the Caribbean.

On the dusty trail

No one disputes that Caribbean coral reefs are dying. An extensive literature, including the comprehensive *Status of Coral Reefs of the World 2000* (edited by Clive Wilkinson and published by the Australian Institute of Marine Science in 2000), documents how anthropogenic threats—overfishing, sedimentation, and direct damage from boats and divers, among others—have combined with elevated sea surface temperatures, pathogens, and hurricanes to severely degrade reef ecosystems around the region. As Ernest Williams and Lucy Bunkley-Williams of the University of Puerto Rico summarize in the September 2000 issue of *The Infectious Disease Review*, the Caribbean has had, by far, the world's most numerous and severe coral reef–associated ecological disturbances. Around the region, diseases and bleaching have decimated once-dominant species like staghorn and elkhorn corals (Acropora cervicornis and A. palmata), longspine sea urchins (Diadema antillarum), and sea fans (Gorgonia spp.). Few species or sites have recovered, and carpets of algae—released from grazing by overfishing and mass mortalities of urchins and other algae-eaters—now dominate many Caribbean reef ecosystems.

Despite extensive research, the demise of Caribbean reefs

has left many scientists frustrated. "We really don't understand why this is happening on a regional level, and it's happening not only in areas where there are a lot of people, it's also happening on remote reefs. Why?" asks Ginger Garrison, a marine ecologist with the US Geological Survey (USGS) field station at Virgin Islands National Park.

> // *Hundreds of millions of tons of African aerosols landing annually in the Caribbean might have major, direct impacts on the region's marine ecosystems.* //

In the 1 October 2000 issue of Geophysical Research Letters ("African Dust and the Demise of Caribbean Coral Reefs," pp. 3029–3032), Gene Shinn, a marine geologist with USGS in St. Petersburg, Florida, and colleagues note the tremendous increase in African dust arriving in the Caribbean beginning in the 1970s. They see more than coincidence in the occurrence of benchmark events in the prolonged, Caribbean-wide decline of coral reefs—such as the arrival of coral black band disease in 1973, mass dieoffs of Acropora corals and Diadema urchins in 1983, along with coral bleaching beginning in 1987—during peak dust years.

"There are just so many things that have happened during this same period of time that the dust levels have been rising. I'm just amazed that people haven't looked at it," says Shinn, who has been studying the effects of oil drilling, sewage spills, and other threats to reefs in the Florida Keys, and watching their continued decline, for decades.

Looking for links

Joseph Prospero, one of the coauthors of "African Dust and the Demise of Caribbean Coral Reefs" and an atmospheric and marine chemist at the University of Miami, has monitored dust deposition in Barbados, at the far eastern edge of the Caribbean, since 1965. His work shows dustfall increasing there in the 1970s following an abrupt shift in the decadal climate cycle known as the North Atlantic Oscillation (NAO). A strengthened NAO led to prolonged drought conditions in the arid Sahel region, on the southern edge of the Sahara desert, as well as easterly trade winds blowing harder across the Atlantic. The changed climate, combined with widespread overgrazing and destructive farming practices in the Sahel, sent vastly greater qualities of exposed soil into the global atmosphere. In peak years, notably during El Niño conditions, winds deposit four times more dust on Barbados than they did before 1970. During the largest dust event ever recorded in February 2000, satellite photos revealed dust forming a continuous bridge from Africa to the Americas. The dust is made up mostly of iron-bearing clays, but it also carries a wide array of living hitchhikers. "The dust is loaded with spores and bacteria," Shinn says. From the first dust sample taken in 1997 by Ginger Garrison, a marine ecologist with the USGS field station at Virgin Islands National Park, researchers at the University of South Carolina now have in culture more than 110 types of bacteria remaining to be identified, as well as a variety of fungal spores. "Conventional wisdom among most microbiologists was that bacteria would be killed by ultraviolet radiation making this five-day trip. But we now know that that's not true, and there are other organisms that can make it," Shinn says. "Swarms of live locusts made it all the way across in 1988 and landed in the Windward Islands. Ships at sea were pelted with locusts. If one-inch grasshoppers can make it, I imagine almost anything can make it."

> **//** *The Caribbean has had, by far, the world's most numerous and severe coral reef–associated ecological disturbances.* **//**

Linking components of the dust to specific diseases is a difficult task—not least because scientists have yet to identify the causative agents for the vast majority of coral reef diseases. In 1996 Garnet Smith of the University of South Carolina and colleagues were able to identify the pathogen behind the mass die-offs of the venus and common sea fans (G. ventalina and G. flabellum) as the soil fungus Aspergillus sydowii. He speculated that widespread deforestation and the ensuing increase in runoff in the Caribbean basin had spread the soil fungus. Not long thereafter, Ginger Garrison sent Smith a sample to see whether the fungus, which does not reproduce in seawater, might be arriving in the air. "We were all absolutely blown away to find out that the very first sample of African dust that I sent him, using all the proper sterile techniques, had Aspergillus sydowii in its pathogenic form," Garrison says.

> *[Marine geologists] see more than coincidence in the occurrence of benchmark [African dust] events in the prolonged, Caribbean-wide decline of coral reefs.*

"We've identified Aspergillus in air samples from both dust and nondust events—not surprising, since Aspergillus is very common," says Julianna Weir, one of Smith's graduate students. (Though the genus is hardly a household name, Aspergillus species include the major killer of people with AIDS, the producer of the carcinogen aflatoxin, and the main ingredient of the digestive aid Beano.) "But we only identified Aspergillus once in a nondust event," she says. Weir, who successfully inoculated healthy venus sea fans with Aspergillus spores cultured from Virgin Island dust samples, emphasizes that "African dust is not the only source of coral pathogens." But her results demonstrate, as she concluded in her talk at the Ninth International Coral Reef Symposium (ICRS) in Bali [in October 2000], that "African dust storms are one way in which pathogens may be introduced into the marine environment." The storms may be the most plausible source of Aspergillus on isolated reefs and near small islands with no forests and little runoff.

Dying Diademas

With other diseases, proponents of the dust hypothesis have had to rely on more circumstantial evidence. Shinn and coauthors speculate that African dust may have caused the largest mass mortality ever recorded of a marine invertebrate, the dieoff of longspine sea urchins. These algae-grazing urchins started dying along the Caribbean coast of Panama in January 1983, a year that brought both a strong El Niño and a major pulse of African dust. Within a year and a half, the mortality front had spread around the Caribbean and western Atlantic. Populations of the urchin, formerly one of the most abundant large invertebrates in the Caribbean, were reduced by 90 percent or more and have made little recovery since.

The prevailing hypothesis is that urchin-killers were somehow transported through the Panama Canal from the Pacific and spread by the main Caribbean current to the east and north. But Shinn and coauthors argue that currents cannot explain the rapid spread of the unknown pathogen to the south—against known currents—through the Windward Islands. They also point to the seasonal pattern of dust events: In the Northern Hemisphere winter, African dust tends to travel to South America and the southern Caribbean; in summer, it heads more for the northern Caribbean and the southeastern United States. "The pattern of seasonal change suggests that a dust-borne pathogen could impact Panama during January and a few months later the entire Caribbean," Shina and colleagues write.

The proposed link between urchin deaths and dust is one of the more controversial parts of the African dust hypothesis. "I have no rival hypothesis for how the Diadema dieoff got started," says Harilaos Lessios, a marine ecologist and leading Diadema researcher with the Smithsonian Tropical Research Institute in Panama. "I kind of like the hypothesis. But the timing is problematic." He observes that if one or two huge dust clouds spread the Diadema pathogen, one would expect to see simultaneous dieoffs over large areas and not, as he and colleagues first documented in the 19 October 1984 issue of *Science*, a mortality front making rapid but distinct advances. Lessios notes too that the Canary and Cape Verde Islands off Africa's Atlantic coast also support populations of Diadema antillarum. Despite the heavy dustings these islands receive, the urchins there have not suffered mass mortality.

The risk of fortified dust

Of course, dust need not carry live organisms to spur outbreaks of pathogens or other opportunistic organisms. It might instead transport nutrients that favor the growth of opportunistic species or help trigger microbes' switch from nonpathogenic to pathogenic forms. African dust is certainly rich in nutrients: Ginger Garrison has found that it is the main source of atmospheric nitrates on the Virgin Island shelf, and it is well known that the dust, by carrying phosphates and other nutrients, supports much of the growth of epiphytes in the Amazon rain forest canopy. Microbiologist Hans Paerl, of the University of North Carolina's Institute of Marine Sciences in Morehead City, says the dust's composition—aluminum, silicon, iron, phosphates, nitrates, and sulfates—makes it like "Geritol for bugs."

Most work on the fertilizing effects of dust in the sea has focused on iron, that essential micronutrient whose chemistry removes it rapidly from seawater. Based in part on experiments in iron-limited areas of the open ocean, proponents suggest that the intense pulses of iron brought by clouds of African dust (which is about 3–6 percent iron) in the Caribbean may be stimulating harmful algal blooms and the rapid growth of both coral-smothering macroalgae and pathogenic microbes. Marshall Hayes, a doctoral candidate in geology at the Duke University Marine Laboratory in Beaufort, North Carolina, has also shown in the lab that doses both of dust and of iron in its more soluble Fe(II) form trigger exponential growth in two types of bacteria that are confirmed coral pathogens.

> *Though iron-laden runoff from lateritic soils of the Caribbean basin reaches many nearshore reefs, . . . pulses of airborne iron may be of more concern for reef health.*

Though iron-laden runoff from lateritic soils of the Caribbean basis reaches many nearshore reefs, Ginger Garrison suggests that the pulses of airborne iron may be of more concern for reef health. Dust events, unlike sedimentation, reach far from shore, and their iron may be more easily taken up by marine organisms. "Just because you have iron locked up in a mineral in a really large particle that hits the water doesn't mean it's available biologically. If you have tiny dust particles where the iron has been first oxidized in the atmosphere, then reduced back to Fe(II), it's hitting the water in a much more available form—chemically and physically—than a big chunk locked up in a clay," Garrison explains.

Yet Alina Szmant of the University of North Carolina at Wilmingon and other critics have questioned the applicability of iron experiments in upwelling zones of the open ocean to coral reefs, with their quite different nutrient availabilities. "There has been very little work on iron in coral reefs," Szmant says. She has observed iron-rich substrates, such as I beams driven into reefs on the Florida Keys and shipwrecks in the Bahamas, where coral recruitment has been enhanced, compared with the surrounding iron-poor substrates. "When you have fresh volcanic surfaces made up of rocks with higher iron content, you tend to get them coated with corals, within just a few years. The algae could get in there too, and can grow faster, but it's the corals that do it," Szmant says.

> ***Caribbean reef researchers . . . [see] the impacts of African dust as an important area of inquiry.*"**

Szmant acknowledges that her observations show only correlation, not a causal connection, between iron content and coral recruitment: "That's the same problem with the dust hypothesis," Szmant argues. "You can say this happened at the same time as that, so this may have caused that, but there could be ten other things that happened as well."

The broader implications

The various organisms and substances found in African dust may have effects on human as well as marine life in the Caribbean. Researchers have only begun to turn their attention to the potential health effects of long-distance aerosols, but they already have some surprising findings. Joseph Prospero says that there is "nothing unusual" about radiation levels of any dust he has sampled, but studies by the USGS's Chuck Holmes suggest that the dust has relatively high concentrations of beryllium-7, a radioactive isotope naturally present in the atmosphere but apparently concentrated on the dust particles in midair. A sample taken from the Mores during the giant dust events of February 2000 emitted gamma radiation at up to 45,000 dpm/g (disintegrations per minute per gram)—roughly three times the radiation allowed in the US workplace, according to Gene Shinn.

Dust researchers have also found pesticides banned for use in the United States mixed in with dust particles too small for human lungs to expel. "When they have locust plagues in Africa, we get chlordane and DDT that we can't use here anymore, but it comes back to us on the wind," Shinn says. "One has to wonder what one-micron-sized particles emitting gamma radiation do when embedded in lung tissue? One could even wonder what it could do to coral tissue once ingested."

While the researchers involved in exploring the potential impacts of African dust are careful to present their work as the basis for a working hypothesis in need of testing, some polluters have already tried to use the hypothesis to sway coral reef management decisions.

"As soon as the African dust theory hit the newspapers in the Florida Keys, the realtors and the developers and everyone who wanted to build up the Keys said, 'See there? We told you. It's not our wastewater. It's not the stormwater runoff. It's African dust.' Well, that comes back to me as a manager, and I have to work on the public relations and sort out what's fact from fiction," says Billy Causey, superintendent of the Florida Keys National Marine Sanctuary.

"When a scientist comes up with a theory, normally the scientific process should take over, and you either prove or disprove the theory," Causey says. "In this instance, people are grasping it as truth and moving forward with making excuses for all the other sins humans have done to coral reefs."

Shinn, who introduced his talk at the ninth ICRS by joking, "I do have my bulletproof vest on in case I need it," has had both scientists and nonscientists misunderstand or outright dismiss his work. "Some people thought we were trying to say that there are no real anthropogenic causes, that it's really this dust, and that's not what I was trying to say," Shinn says. "The dust is added on top of all these other problems."

Like many Caribbean reef researchers, Alina Szmant sees the impacts of African dust as an important area of inquiry but is withholding judgment until more results come in. "I think the value of a hypothesis like this is it gets a lot of people thinking and a lot of people doing work. It may be right, it may not be right, but that's part of the process of science. You don't always have to be right when you come up with a really great new idea."

8

Tourism Threatens Coral Reefs

United Nations Environment Programme

The United Nations Environment Programme sponsors research and shares information to encourage nations to adopt sustainable development policies.

Tourism-related activities impact coral reefs directly and indirectly. Some of the direct effects are physical damage to the reef by careless snorkelers and divers, and boaters who run aground on the coral. More seriously, however, are the indirect impacts of tourism. Tourism increases coastal construction, and the resulting sediment covers the coral, making it difficult for coral to get the light it needs. Increased sewage pollution and recreational fuel spills also put stress on struggling coral reef life. Governments must prevent or reduce these threats to protect any coral reefs on which tourism-dependent communities depend.

Coral reefs are under threat, suffering from decline and degradation due to a combination of natural and anthropogenic factors. The scientific community is in agreement about it and the press talks about it. Fifty-eight percent of the world's reefs are potentially threatened by human activity. Overexploitation and coastal development pose the greatest potential threat.

Assessments made in late 2000 show that 27% of the world's reefs have been effectively lost, with the largest single cause being the massive climate-related coral bleaching event of 1998. This destroyed about 16% of the coral reefs of the world in 9 months dur-

United Nations Environment Programme, "An Ecosystem Under Threat," www.uneptie.org, March 22, 2002. Copyright © 2002 by the United Nations Environment Programme. Reproduced by permission.

ing the largest El Niño and La Niña climate events ever recorded.

Some of the man-made damage is related to tourism. At the same time, tourism is of great economic importance to countries with significant areas of coral reef, such as the Caribbean states and territories. For some smaller island territories, tourism is the mainstay of the local economy. Because tourism in the Caribbean is dependent almost entirely on coastal resources, most development takes place in the coastal zone and most of the impacts occur in the coastal zone. Impacts from tourism activities include both direct physical impacts (such as diver damage and anchor damage), as well as indirect impacts from resort development and operation, and development of tourism infrastructure in general.

Impacts from tourism can often be reduced by raising awareness and changing behaviour among both tourists and local tourism industry workers.

The tourism impacts on coral reefs

The tourism-related impacts on coral reefs in the Caribbean are typical of those occurring worldwide. The tourism sector is of major economic importance in the Caribbean region, both for foreign exchange earnings and for employment. Since Caribbean tourism is primarily associated with beaches and the sea, there have been—and continue to be—impacts from tourism on the coastal environment, including the coral reefs.

> *Tourism has both direct and indirect impacts on coral reefs.*

Tourism has both direct and indirect impacts on coral reefs. Snorkeling, diving and boating can cause direct physical damage to reefs, and fishing and collecting can contribute to over-exploitation of reef species and threaten local survival of endangered species. Indirect impacts relate to the development, construction and operation of tourism infrastructure as a whole (resorts, marines, ports, airports, etc.).

Direct physical damage from snorkeling and diving has been the subject of extensive study and is well documented. The damage inflicted by divers and snorkelers consists mostly of breaking fragile, branched corals or causing lesions to massive corals. Most divers and snorkelers cause little damage; only a few cause severe or widespread damage. Research indicates that reef degradation and change of reef community structure occurs once a certain level of use by divers and snorkelers is exceeded. As a rule of thumb it is recommended that the level of 5,000 to 6,000 dives per sites per year should not be exceeded. Training and briefing of divers and snorkelers will greatly help to reduce negative impacts.

> *The damage inflicted by divers and snorkelers consists mostly of breaking fragile, branched corals or causing lesions to massive corals.*

Physical damage from anchors and especially boat groundings can be severe. Anchor damage is proportional to the size of the boat (i.e. weight of the anchor and length of anchor chain) and is further dependent on the type of coral community. Recovery of coral damage from boat groundings is slow. Anchor damage can be avoided to a large extent by installing permanent moorings, designating anchorages and providing adequate information on anchoring and mooring.

Although fishing has caused declines in reef fish stocks throughout the Caribbean, the *direct* role of tourism in fishing-related decline is most likely not significant. Indirectly, however, tourism increases the demand for seafood and does have an impact on reef fish resources. Collecting of marine souvenirs by tourists is probably insignificant but there still is a market for marine curiosities in response to a certain tourist demand. This demand can definitely be decreased by increased awareness.

Tourism generates more sewage

Tourism-related sources of sewage pollution include resorts and, to a much lesser extent, recreational vessels. There is evidence that a very large percentage of the sewage generated by hotels is discharged in coastal waters without adequate treatment. The main impact of sewage pollution is nutrient enrichment, which favours certain species (algae in particular) at the expense of corals. The impacts of nutrient enrichment from sewage pollution on corals in general have been well studied, but those specifically from sewage pollution from hotels and recreational vessels have not been quantified. The studies indicate that the impact of sewage pollution depends on the level of treatment before discharge and the degree of natural flushing by tides and currents at the point of discharge.

Tourism is not generally a source of petroleum hydrocarbon pollution, other than on a small scale when oil or fuel spills from recreational vessels and marines occur. The effects of petroleum hydrocarbons on corals has been studied for quite some time, producing evidence that chronic oil pollution is more harmful than a single exposure, and that dispersants and emulsifiers used to combat spills are more toxic to corals than oil alone.

Coastal development and the construction and operation of related tourism infrastructure cause increased runoff and sedimentation. Sedimentation is one of the main reasons for reef degradation. Increased sediment loading of coastal waters increases turbidity, reduces light levels and leads to stress on corals, usually expressed by "bleaching" of corals. Heavy sediment loading may also cause corals to suffocate and die. Other documented impacts of sedimentation on corals include lower growth rates, reduced productivity and reduced recruitment.

Tourism is obviously a source of large amounts of solid waste, the impacts of which depend very much on the method of disposal. If disposed of inappropriately, leaching of toxic substances may harm corals. Of particular concern is the "accidental" waste—plastics in particular—that is blown into the ocean from beaches or vessels and has a detrimental effect on corals and other marine life.

Tourism-related impacts on coral reefs are significant, but they are also compounded by other impacts that are not easily distinguished from those of tourism. This does not mean that we must disregard the impacts of tourism activities. On the contrary, the tourism sector and government agencies involved in tourism development must try to eliminate or reduce those impacts that can be controlled, even if there is no 100% proof that a certain impact is directly related to a tourist activity.

9

Trade in Coral Organisms Threatens Coral Reefs

Andrew W. Bruckner

Andrew W. Bruckner is a coral reef ecologist in the National Marine Fisheries Service's Office of Protected Resource in Silver Spring, Maryland.

Increased trade in coral reef organisms for jewelry, curios, and aquariums is threatening coral reefs. Increased demand for aquarium fish has led to destructive fishing practices such as cyanide fishing, which is killing reef life. Moreover, the harvesting of coral erodes the reefs that protect coastlines. The United States regulates the harvesting of coral in its own reefs, yet to meet the demand for aquarium coral, it imports coral from foreign markets, threatening foreign reefs. Although much more attention has been focused on pollution, global warming, and overfishing as major culprits in destroying the coral reefs, consumer trade can no longer be overlooked.

C oral reef ecosystems are a valuable source of food and income to coastal communities around the world. Yet destructive human activities have now put nearly 60 percent of the world's coral reefs in jeopardy, according to a 1998 World Resources Institute study. Pollution and sediments from agriculture and industry and overexploitation of fishery resources are the biggest problems, but the fragility of reef ecosystems means that even less damaging threats can no longer be ignored. Prominent among these is the harvest of coral, fish, and

Andrew W. Bruckner, "New Threat to Coral Reefs: Trade in Coral Organisms," *Issues in Science and Technology Online*, Fall 2000. Copyright © 2000 by the University of Texas at Dallas, Richardson, TX. Reproduced by permission.

other organisms for the aquarium, jewelry, and curio trades, as well as live fish for restaurants. Much of the demand comes from the United States, which has made protecting coral reefs a top priority.

A growing interest worldwide

International trade in marine fishes and some invertebrates has gone on for decades, but the growing popularity of reef aquaria has increased the types and the quantity of species in trade. More than 800 species of reef fish and hundreds of coral species and other invertebrates are now exported for aquarium markets. The vast majority of fish come from reefs in the Philippines and Indonesia—considered to be the world's most biologically diverse marine areas—and most stony coral comes from Indonesia. But the commercial harvest of ornamental reef fish and invertebrates (other than stony coral) occurs on reefs worldwide, including those under U.S. jurisdiction. In 1985, the world export value of the marine aquarium trade was estimated at $25 million to $40 million per year. Since 1985, trade in marine ornamentals has been increasing at an average rate of 14 percent annually. In 1996, the world export value was about $200 million. The annual export of marine aquarium fish from Southeast Asia alone is, according to 1997 data, between 10 million and 30 million fish with a retail value of up to $750 million.

> *More than 800 species of reef fish and hundreds of coral [reef] species and other invertebrates are now exported for aquarium markets.*

Although there are no firm estimates of the impact that trade is having on overall coral reef health, it is unlikely that it is minimal, as some believe. Indeed, although the diversity, standing stock, and yield of coral reef resources are extremely high, most coral reef fisheries have not been sustainable for long when commercially exploited. Indonesia, the world's largest exporter of coral reef organisms, is a case in point. Because of overfishing and destructive practices such as using cyanide to stun fish for capture, coral mining, and blast fishing, only 5 to 7 percent of Indonesia's reefs were estimated in 1996 to have excellent coral cover. Unfortunately, however, because of the growing international demand for aquarium organisms and live food fish, overharvesting in nearshore waters has simply pushed commercial ventures to expand their harvesting into more remote ocean locations.

> **//** *As the world's largest importer of coral reef organisms for curios, jewelry, and aquariums, the United States has a major responsibility to address the damage to coral reef ecosytems. //*

As the world's largest importer of coral reef organisms for curios, jewelry, and aquariums, the United States has a major responsibility to address the damage to coral reef ecosystems that arises from commerce in coral reef species. The United States took a critical first step in 1999 by approving a plan to conserve coral reefs, which included strategies to promote the sustainable use of coral reefs worldwide. The plan identified unsustainable harvesting of reef organisms for U.S. markets as a major source of concern. Now we need to adopt some concrete steps to put that plan into action.

Increasing exploitation

The group of organisms commonly known as stony corals consists of animal polyps that secrete a calcareous skeleton. They are used locally for building materials, road construction, and the production of lime and are traded internationally for sale as souvenirs, jewelry, and aquarium organisms. Corals in trade may be live specimens, skeletons, or "live rock," which is coral skeletons and coralline algae with other coral reef organisms attached. Live rock, often broken out of the reef with crowbars, is reef structure; removing it harms or destroys habitat for other species. Extraction of stony corals and live rock is known to increase erosion, destroy habitat, and reduce biodiversity. It is likely that the destruction of coral reef ecosystems will continue unless conservation efforts are improved.

Statistics on the type and number of coral reef specimens in trade, the source, and the importer have been available since

1985, thanks to the Convention on International Trade in Endangered Species of Wild Fauna and Flora (CITES). All stony corals, including live rock, are listed in Appendix II of CITES. Commercial trade in Appendix II species is permitted under CITES, provided that the exporting country finds that the take does not constitute a significant risk to the species in the wild or its role in the ecosystem.

> **//** *The marine aquarium trade possesses a major potential for overexploitation [of coral reefs] because fish collectors capture large quantities of particular species.* **//**

The stony coral trade is dominated by exports from Southeast Asia and the South Pacific. The United States either prohibits or strictly limits the harvest of stony corals in most of its own waters because of the key role that corals play in the ecosystem and because of widespread concern that the organisms are vulnerable to overexploitation. But the lucrative U.S. market remains open to foreign coral, and thousands of shipments arrive yearly from Indonesia, Fiji, and other nations. Indonesia exports approximately 900,000 stony corals each year. Fiji is the primary supplier of live rock and the second largest exporter of stony coral, with a trade that has doubled or tripled in volume each year for the past five years. In 1997, more than 600 metric tons of live rock was harvested from Fijian reefs, 95 percent of it destined for the United States.

A change in the market

Until about a decade ago, more than 90 percent of the corals harvested for international markets were sold for decoration; these were harvested live, bleached and cleaned to remove tissue, and exported as skeletons. Although the trade in coral skeletons has remained fairly constant since 1993, the volume of live specimens for the aquarium trade has grown at a rate of 12 percent to 30 percent per year during the 1990s. In 1997, live coral constituted more than half of the global trade.

Aquarium specimens are typically fist-sized colonies that represent six months to ten years of growth, depending on the type of coral. Most often, these are slow-growing, massive species with large fleshy polyps, many of which are uncommon or are vulnerable to overexploitation because of their life history characteristics. The flowerpot coral (*Goniopora*) and the anchor (or hammer) coral (*Euphyllia spp.*) are the most abundant corals in trade, partly because they must be continually replaced. These species survive poorly in captivity. They are also easily damaged during collection, are susceptible to disease, and acclimate badly to artificial conditions.

The preferred corals for the curio market are "branching" species. These grow faster than most corals destined for the aquarium trade; however, they are traded at a significantly larger size. Colonies in trade are often more than a meter in diameter, representing a decade or more of growth. In addition, these species are most susceptible to crown-of-thorns sea star predation, physical damage from storms, and bleaching. Bleaching is a response to stress, particularly elevated seawater temperature, in which corals expel energy-producing symbiotic algae. Coral can survive bleaching but usually do so in a weakened state. In 1998, coral reefs around the world experienced the most extensive bleaching in the modern record. In many locations, 70 to 90 percent of all corals bleached and subsequently died; branching corals sustained the highest mortality. Continued extraction of these species at current levels may reduce the ability of coral reefs to recover from disturbances such as bleaching.

The impact on fish

Destructive fishing practices and overexploitation of certain fish species are having significant effects on populations of coral reef fish and other organisms, as well as on reef ecosystems. Nearly 25,000 metric tons of reef fish are harvested alive each year for the fish food trade, with an annual retail value of about $1 billion. Unfortunately, cyanide fishing is the preferred method for capturing these fish, and currently at least 10 key exporting countries use it. One of the most deadly poisons known, cyanide usually only stuns the fish, but it destroys coral reef habitat by poisoning and killing non-target animals, including corals. Other chemicals, including quinaldine and plant toxins, are also used to capture reef fish alive. Field data on these practices are hard to come by because they are illegal, and thus fishers are secretive about them.

Destructive fishing practices probably figure in the high mortality rate of organisms while they are in transit. A 1997 survey of U.S. retailers found that between one-third to more than half of the aquarium fish imported from Southeast Asia died shortly after arrival. No conclusive studies on the reasons have yet been published, but these deaths are believed to be due to the poisons used in capture or the stress of handling and transport, or both. The need for replacements is one factor that keeps demand high and thus contributes to overexploitation.

Compounding the threats posed by cyanide fishing, over-exploitation of ornamental fishes can lead to depletion of target species and may alter the ecology of the reef community. The marine aquarium trade possesses a major potential for overexploitation because fish collectors capture large quantities of particular species. Herbivorous surgeonfish are one of the primary targets. These fish are a critical component of a healthy coral reef ecosystem, because, along with parrotfish, they control the algae population; unchecked, algae can overgrow stony corals and inhibit settlement and growth of coral larvae. Fishers also tend to capture the smaller young fish before they can reproduce. In some cases, aquarium fish collectors are in direct competition with subsistence fishers, because several fish species captured as juveniles for the aquarium trade are also commercially important food fish. Studies have only recently begun to document the extent and potential impact of collection for the aquarium trade on reef fish populations. For instance, in Kona, Hawaii, five of the top aquarium fish species were 45 to 63 percent less abundant in areas where tropical reef fish collection is allowed.

Efforts to improve conservation

Several exporting countries have recognized the potential threats associated with the coral trade and have taken steps to address them. Mozambique, for example, banned the trading of coral skeletons and stony corals because of excess harvest rates and the high death rates that occurred during the 1998 bleaching. The Philippines implemented a total ban on coral trading after studies found that areas of intensive coral harvest exhibited a reduced abundance and altered size distribution of commercially collected coral species. From the combination of intensive coral collection, cyanide use, and blast fishing, several Philippine reefs became barren. To reverse this trend, the country has established a pilot program to conserve coral reef resources while allowing nondestructive sustainable collection. The Philippine government and the International Marinelife Alliance have implemented an aggressive program to retrain fishers in alternatives to cyanide, such as using nets for aquarium fishes and hook and line for food fishes. Five cyanide-detection facilities have also been established. After five years of intensive efforts, live reef fish that test positive for cyanide have declined from 80 percent to less than 30 percent.

> **⁄⁄** *From the combination of intensive coral collection, cyanide use, and blast fishing, several Philippine [coral] reefs became barren.* **⁄⁄**

Instead of banning coral collection, Australia has developed an effective management strategy designed to ensure sustainability of the resource. Coral reef habitats have been zoned for different uses, including no-take areas. Collectors are licensed, and the collection of coral is permitted only in selected areas that amount to less than 1 percent of the reefs in a region. Collectors have harvested 45 to 50 metric tons of coral per year for 20 years, with no noticeable impact on the resource.

Hawaii has established a regional fishery management area along the west coast of the Big Island. As of January 2000, a minimum of 30 percent of the nearshore waters were designated as fish replenishment areas where collection of aquarium fish is prohibited. The Marine Aquarium Council (MAC), on behalf of hobbyists, the industry, and some environmental groups, is developing a certification scheme that will track an animal from collector to hobbyist. The goals of MAC are to develop standards for quality products and sustainable practices and a system to certify compliance with these standards and to create consumer demand for certified products.

Recognizing the power of the United States to shape the reef trade, a presidential executive order established the U.S. Coral Reef Task Force in 1998. Its purpose is to lead U.S. efforts to protect and enhance coral reef ecosystems. The task force, composed of the leaders of 11 federal agencies and the governors of states, territories, and commonwealths with coral reefs, found that more than 80 percent of the stony coral and nearly

50 percent of marine aquarium fish in trade during the 1990s were destined for U.S. ports and that international trade is increasing by 10 to 20 percent each year.

The task force has identified several key actions to reduce impacts associated with the trade. These include training and education programs, guidelines for sustainable management and best handling practices, and improved data collection and monitoring to ensure that the growing harvest of ornamental coral reef organisms is sustainable.

10

Fishing Bans to Protect Coral Reefs Should Be Expanded

Keay Davidson

Keay Davidson, a science journalist, writes for magazines such as Scientific American, New Scientist, *and* National Geographic. *He also authored the biography* Carl Sagan: A Life.

Experts warn that if nothing is done to protect them from overfishing, coral reefs will not survive. Thus "no-take zones" that ban fishing should be expanded. Historical evidence shows that overfishing leads to the destruction of coral reef ecosystems because coral reef species depend on one another to survive; the extinction of one species leads to the loss of another until eventually the ecosystem itself collapses. This devastation in turn harms communities that depend on the reef for survival. While some governments such as the United States have implemented fishing bans to protect some coral reef ecosystems, more bans should be enacted worldwide.

Pummeled by overfishing, the world's coral reef ecosystems "will not survive for more than a few decades" unless drastic action is taken to protect them, experts warn.

To forestall a disaster that could devastate marine life, expose populous coastlines to stormier waves and economically devastate a tourism-dependent nation like Australia, the United States and other nations should vastly expand the designated "no-

take" zones—where fishing and other exploitation is banned—
in coral ecosystems, said one author of an article [for the August
15, 2003] issue of *Science*.

Historical evidence dating back thousands of years proves
that overfishing, not recent coral diseases or other causes, is the
main cause of the slow death of the world's coral ecosystems,
marine paleontologist John Pandolfi of the Smithsonian's National Museum of Natural History and 11 other researchers say
in the article.

"Overfishing seems to be the largest 'signal' that explains
our data," Pandolfi said.

Another co-author, marine ecologist Enric Sala of Scripps
Institution of Oceanography in La Jolla [California] said,
"What we're seeing in coral reefs is something akin to turning
a tropical jungle into a golf course."

So far they've documented only one out-and-out extinction of a coral reef inhabitant—the Caribbean monk seal. But
over the centuries, many outer coral reef denizens have declined to the point where they have "no ecological impact—
they're functionally 'gone,' like coral trout, snapper, many of
the turtles, (and) the manatees," Pandolfi said.

Because coral ecosystem life forms are so interdependent,
the continual loss of species "is like taking bricks out of a building, one by one. At a certain point the building is going to
come crashing down," he added. "There are places like Jamaica
where the percentage of live coral (as opposed to dead coral) is
down to 5 percent."

> **❝** *The United States and other nations should
> vastly expand the designated 'no-take' zones . . . in
> coral ecosystems.* **❞**

As moviegoers who've seen *Finding Nemo* know, a coral reef
"provides a lot of places for fish to live. Coral reefs occupy
about 0.2 percent of the world's oceans, yet they contain 25
percent of the species diversity," Pandolfi said.

For fish, coral reefs are combination condos and restaurants. They're attractive to fish partly because they provide
shelter from predators and all the food they can swallow. They
also offer numerous idiosyncratic ecological "niches" for those

oddball fish—the loners and bohemians of the undersea world—who prefer to, say, burrow into the sand beneath the coral rather than hobnob within the coral complex itself.

Ever since humans began fishing thousands of years ago, species that jam the undersea metropolises called coral ecosystems have been gradually disappearing—the biggest species first, such as green turtles—according to the researchers' analysis of historical and archaeological records.

They pored over documents such as Colonial-era records of fish catches from 14 coral reef ecosystems in the Atlantic and Pacific oceans and Red Sea, including Australia's Great Barrier Reef and coral reefs of the Caribbean.

> *Based on the historical records, overfishing should be targeted as the No. 1 cause of coral ecosystem decline.*

One of the 12 co-authors, zoology Professor Karen A. Bjorndal of the University of Florida, and her colleagues found more than 400 documents, some of them going back to the British colonial era and earlier, that recorded fish catches over the centuries in the Bahamas alone. They learned that native Bahamians severely depleted the coral ecosystem's green turtles long before the Brits arrived.

"I used to think that green turtles were basically in pristine shape when Columbus arrived (in Bahama five centuries ago), and I don't think that anymore," Bjorndal said in a press release issued by the university.

Based on the historical records, overfishing should be targeted as the No. 1 cause of coral ecosystem decline, the scientists concluded.

As an analogy, "imagine if 90 percent of the redwoods disappeared in Northern California," Sala said.

No-take zones need to be expanded

One solution: No-take zones should be greatly expanded in the world's coral ecosystems, Pandolfi said in a phone interview. The U.S. government has already designated five percent of coral ecosystems under its control as no-take zones. But Pandolfi advocates boosting the percentage to as high as 50 percent.

Pandolfi cites a legal precedent: The state of California's recent move to greatly expand protection to marine ecosystems off its coast. [During 2002 and 2003], the California state Fish and Game Commission boosted to 11 percent the no-take share of the 1,500-square-mile Channel islands National Marine Sanctuary off Santa Barbara and Ventura. The previous percentage was less than ½₀ of one percent, according to ocean environmental activists.

Besides threatening the food supply of much of the world, reef loss could imperil natural harbors that are sheltered by coral formation and could undermine tourism based on the appeal of vibrant coral life.

Failure to prevent continued coral reef deterioration could turn countries such as Australia—which are dependent on tourism at attractions such as the Great Barrier Reef—into "Third World countries," Pandolfi said.

Some anti-environmentalists might scoff, saying that humanity will continue to muddle through whatever happens to the coral reefs, Pandolfi acknowledged. He added: "If you want to live in a world where the ocean is mostly jellyfish and bacteria, there's nothing I can do about it."

11

Fishing and Boating Bans May Not Protect Coral Reefs

Ryck Lydecker

Ryck Lydecker is vice president of the Boat Owners Association of the United States, an organization that promotes the rights of boaters.

Banning fishing by expanding the percentage of U.S. coral reefs designated as "no-take" marine reserves is not the right approach to protecting coral reefs. Recreational fishing advocates argue that other methods such as seasonal and size limits adequately protect reefs from overfishing. Some experts claim that the harm to coral reefs from recreational fishing and diving is insignificant when compared to the harm that results from other human activities, such as cyanide fishing and agriculture, and from natural threats, such as hurricanes and reef disease. By expanding no-take reserves, environmental advocates alienate the people most interested in conservation—fishermen.

Four years ago, scientists studying coral reefs in the Caribbean Sea made a startling discovery. Analyzing meteorological records from Barbados, they noted that episodes of coral deaths coincided perfectly with those years in which high levels of airborne dust settled over the region.

The dust, it turns out, blows off the Sahara Desert and nearly one billion tons of it ride the prevailing winds across the Atlantic Ocean from Africa to the Caribbean each year. The

Ryck Lydecker, "Quandary over Coral Reefs," *Boat/U.S. Magazine*, vol. 5, July 2000. Copyright © 2000 by Ryck Lydecker. Reproduced by permission.

dust contains compounds and organisms that are damaging and probably killing the living coral.

What most people think of as coral are the limestone formations secreted by tiny living organisms related to the sea anemone. There are several hundred species of these animals, called polyps, and the reef colonies they build are found in shallow, tropical marine waters roughly between 30 degrees north and 30 degrees south of the equator.

Millions of polyps can comprise a typical reef ecosystem, along with all the related marine life and fish that make up the food web, but living coral reefs as a whole cover only about one percent of the world's ocean floor. That could change dramatically, according to . . . estimates, because a wide variety of natural and human-induced causes threaten to wipe out as much as 70% of these reefs by the year 2050. But recent proposals to help solve the problem of worldwide coral destruction by putting U.S. reefs off-limits to anglers and boaters are now raising a different kind of dust.

> *The idea of excluding recreational fishing when other measures [to protect coral reefs] can be taken is wrong.*

In its National Action Plan to Conserve Coral Reefs, . . . the presidentially appointed U.S. Coral Reef Task Force recommended that a "bare minimum" of 20% of all coral reefs in U.S. waters—some 840,000 acres—be set aside over the next 10 years as "marine wilderness" or "marine replenishment zones" in which recreational as well as commercial fishing would be prohibited.

Some fishing and boating industry observers fear such restrictions could extend to all types of boating as well as to diving or other water sports. Catch-and-release fishing on these reefs and even trolling over them for non reef-dwelling game fish also could be prohibited.

Trouble in paradise

"Protecting 20% of U.S. coral reefs and other actions called for in the plan are crucial because two-thirds of the world's reefs may be dying," reports Dr. D. James Baker, administrator of the National Oceanic and Atmospheric Administration (NOAA). Baker is co-chairman of the task force, created by President [Bill] Clinton in June 1999 by executive order. The task force is made up of representatives of 12 federal agencies including the Department of Interior, which has jurisdiction over reefs in national parks, and NOAA, which manages 13 national marine sanctuaries off U.S. coasts and regulates fishing in federal waters beyond three miles.

> *Natural phenomena like hurricanes and disease pose greater threats to coral reefs than sport fishing.*

Due to the vast diversity of plant and animal life that makes up coral reef ecosystems, they are now being referred to as "the rain forests of the sea" and environmentalists say they are as desperately in need of protection as the world's beleaguered tropical forest belt. Numerous national and international environmental groups are starting to beat the "save the reefs" drum.

Hawaii has some 86% of all coral reefs in U.S. waters. The rest are found in the Florida Keys, the Gulf of Mexico, the U.S. Virgin Islands and in the Pacific Trust territories of Guam, Samoa and the Northern Mariana Islands.

[As of July 2000], only 5% of all reefs are adequately mapped and the task force plan calls for completing the job by 2009. It also recommends establishing a national monitoring system to keep tabs on the health of the reefs and the fish that inhabit them. In addition, the plan calls for restoring damaged reefs and for stepped-up enforcement of regulations governing trade in hard corals and reef fishes for the aquarium market.

In the Caribbean, according to the National Marine Fisheries Service, more than 20% of reef-dependent species are considered over-fished, while in Hawaii the most abundant reef fish populations have declined by 40% in the past two decades.

Citing those kinds of numbers, the task force called for identifying the most important coral reef habitats and spawning populations of reef fish in U.S. waters to be included in the network of "no-take" marine reserves.

But is putting 20% of U.S. reefs off-limits to fishing the right approach?

"Absolutely not," says Mike Nussman, vice president of the American Sportfishing Association (www.asafishing.org). "The 20% is an arbitrary number and there is no science to back it up.

"Of course we are in favor of protecting marine resources where it's warranted," Nussman says. "But the idea of excluding recreational fishing when other measures can be taken is wrong.

"If the goal is to restore overfished species, there are proven management tools like bag limits, seasons and size limits that will do the job," Nussman says. "Setting zones that keep everyone out is not necessarily good management."

Coral costs

With a touch of irony not lost on members of the fishing and boating industries, the task force portrays the value of reefs in human economic terms. It notes that in U.S. waters, coral reefs generate millions of jobs and support a $100 million annual commercial fishing industry.

The task force report puts the value of most coral reef ecosystems in the "billions of dollars" based on court-approved assessments to repair damaged reefs and "lost tourism use." Such assessments can reach over $2,800 per square meter of reef.

Although fishing and shellfish harvesting are permitted in some fashion on all reefs in federal waters, closing 20% is necessary, the task force maintains, to prevent the over-fishing of reef-dependent species. It is also necessary to prevent damage to the fragile reefs themselves from vessel anchoring, scuba diving, spear fishing and coral scavenging.

The task force estimates 10% of reefs worldwide have already been lost and 60% are directly threatened by human activities. Harm from recreational fishing, Nussman says, pales in comparison with other coral-killing factors cited in the report, including shoreline development, runoff from farm-land, over-harvesting of coral for the aquarium trade, destructive fishing practices and ship groundings. In some parts of the world, fishermen have been known to dynamite reefs or poison the water around them to kill or stun the fish.

Natural phenomena like hurricanes and disease pose greater threats to coral reefs than sport fishing, Nussman says. In fact, he sees the coral reef initiative as the camel's nose under the tent in a much broader effort to establish ocean and near-shore "marine protected areas" or "marine reserves."

He cites growing efforts by various environmental organizations to establish no-take zones beyond coral reefs, in the coastal waters of national parks and wildlife refuges, ostensibly to help restore overfished stocks.

"Rebuilding the ocean's depleted fisheries is a 10-year effort," Nussman says. "Today there are numerous environmental organizations pushing for changes in marine fisheries management but it's not very exciting waiting for the stocks to rebuild. These organizations have to have something to do.

"There's a push for marine protected areas all over now and it's an easy issue to sound-bite," he adds. "You can make people in Kansas think that the answer to fisheries restoration is to keep anglers out. But public access is what drives recreational fishing and if you take that away, you are going to lose the most important constituency for conservation there is, the anglers themselves."

President [Bill] Clinton issued an Executive Order May 26 [2000] calling for stronger regulations in existing marine protected areas while expanding the system throughout coastal ocean and Great Lakes waters.

12

Satellite Imaging Helps Scientists Study Threatened Coral Reefs

Brian Soliday

Brian Soliday is executive vice president of sales and market-ing at Space Imaging in Thornton, Colorado.

National Oceanic and Atmospheric Administration (NOAA) scientists can monitor coral reefs from space using high-resolution satellite images. In order to mon-itor reef health and come up with effective manage-ment strategies, NOAA scientists need detailed, quanti-tative data to determine what factors contribute to reef degradation. Reef locations are often remote, however, and obtaining detailed information on overall reef health has been difficult. Trained divers can obtain in-formation for local studies, but large-scale studies are expensive. With satellite images, NOAA can map entire reefs and more accurately determine the impact of hu-man and natural activities on these fragile ecosystems.

When most people think of coral reefs, they envision unique types of fish, lobsters, and other exotic marine creatures inhabiting clear blue water in a beautiful, brightly col-ored environment. While this image is generally valid, it may soon be no more than a memory if current trends continue. Over the years, the health of coral reefs around the globe has deteriorated severely, as a result of both human and natural abuse. This situation has become a major concern, especially among scientists, because the reefs are more than just aesthetically pleasing marine habitats; they are the most biologically diverse of all marine communities and are vital for survival of the larger ecosystem.

On a recent trip to Jamaica, I observed firsthand the problems facing coral reef habitats. While snorkeling along the beautiful coasts, I noticed that the reefs looked different in various sections of the waters. Although many reefs farther from the coastline appeared healthy, those nearer the coast were in a state of decline or obviously devastated.

> **"** *Why not use high-resolution satellite imagery to study and map coral reef locations?* **"**

As I surveyed the damage, I clearly saw the need to protect these unique but fragile ecosystems. It brought to mind a project that Space Imaging (the company I work for) is currently involved in to help preserve these valuable natural resources. The work is being done in collaboration with Steve Rohmann, a physical scientist at the Special Projects Office of the National Oceanic and Atmospheric Administration (NOAA).

Last year [2000], Rohmann approached Space Imaging with an unusual suggestion: Why not use high-resolution satellite imagery to study and map coral reef locations? At first, the idea seemed farfetched. How could a satellite more than 400 miles in space collect detailed pictures of objects underwater? As we explored the idea together, I learned more about the state of coral reef health worldwide and the difficulty and expense of studying reefs with traditional methods. It was exciting to observe Space Imaging technicians working with a brilliant team of scientists at NOAA in the process of discovering how to see underwater with an orbiting Earth.

Threats to reef habitats

In working with Rohmann, I found out that coral reefs play an important role in the survival of various forms of marine life and hold practical benefits for humans as well. They serve as habitats for fish and other sea animals and plants, and they protect coastlines from storm damage and erosion. They provide needed food to local communities and help generate billions of dollars in tourism revenue, creating jobs. Many coastal regions in the United States and abroad are economically dependent on coral reefs and would be devastated if their decline continued.

Moreover, a number of lifesaving medicines—such as treatments for cancer, arthritis, and certain bacterial and viral infections—can also be derived from the reefs. Yet, despite all the ways in which these coral reefs benefit humans, we knowingly and unknowingly contribute to their deterioration.

Under normal conditions, a healthy coral reef is able to recover from natural disturbances, such as hurricanes or other tropical storms, within approximately 10 to 20 years. But when it is subjected to chronic, human-induced stress, recovery can be almost impossible.

One of the main problems is pollution, as damage is caused by everything from oil spills to chemical runoff. Certain types of pollution, such as from fertilizers and untreated sewage, create dangerously elevated levels of algae in coral reef habitats. Typically, fish and marine invertebrates eat enough of the algae to keep the nutrient level normal, but at high concentrations, the algae can overwhelm and smother the coral polyps.

> *Without detailed maps, quantitative assessment of the factors causing coral reef decline can be difficult or even impossible.*

Another serious threat occurs in the form of fishing, because dynamite, cyanide, and bleach are commonly used to catch fish in these areas. Between 1986 and 1991, approximately half the coral reefs in the Philippines were destroyed by such methods. Besides going after tropical fish, fishermen target a variety of exotic animals—including conch and lobsters—that live in coral reefs. Negligent handling of nets, lines, and traps often leads to coral reef damage, and overharvesting the various creatures could cause them to become extinct. In addition, heavy boat traffic can cause significant damage, as carelessly dropped anchors often crush sections of the reef.

Then again, human fascination with various types of coral has made them popular as tourist souvenirs. And there is a worldwide market for their use in aquarium decorations, jewelry, and other items.

Developing protective measures

NOAA and other government agencies have been studying coral reefs for many years, and they have made it a top priority to help protect these vital natural resources. According to a recent report published by the Global Coral Reef Monitoring Network, as much as 10 percent of the world's reefs are already dead, and another 30 percent may be dead by the year 2050. To help find a solution to this problem, former president [Bill] Clinton issued an executive order on June 11, 1998, establishing the U.S. Coral Reef Task Force. This task force is responsible for overseeing and implementing the intent of the executive order, namely, to "preserve and protect the biodiversity, health, heritage, and social and economic value of U.S. coral reef ecosystems and the marine environment."

Rohmann knew that accurate maps are critical for the study, protection, and management of coral reefs. Scientists need them to observe how the reefs change over time. But without detailed maps, quantitative assessment of the factors causing coral reef decline can be difficult or even impossible. He therefore saw the need for new technologies to generate such maps.

High-resolution satellite imagery offered by Space Imaging had been widely used to photograph and study features such as rivers, mountains, roads, bridges, agricultural fields, and so on, but it had not been successfully tested underwater. Rohmann believed, however, that Space Imaging's IKONOS satellite (launched in September 1999) could be used to obtain highly detailed images of large areas of shallow-water coral reef ecosystems, and that it would be more efficient to obtain images with this technology than with imaging technologies used previously.

> *Earlier methods to gather data about coral reefs included aerial photography and reconnaissance dives by trained personnel.*

Earlier methods to gather data about coral reefs included aerial photography and reconnaissance dives by trained personnel. While the level of detail obtained with these methods can be useful for localized studies of individual reefs or sections thereof, both are cost—and labor—intensive for large-scale studies of reef ecosystems. It is expensive to process and generate maps from aerial images, and it can be tough to maneuver airplanes in certain areas or provide enough reserve fuel for a successful mission. In addition, human divers have limited access to some parts of reefs.

> *High-resolution satellite imagery may also prove useful for assessing the impact of hazardous material spills and ship groundings on coral reefs.*

In the case of some well-known coral reefs, such as the Great Barrier Reef of Australia, large sections have been mapped. But because marine environments are far more difficult to chart than land areas, there are few detailed maps for the vast majority of the world's coral reefs, such as those in the Indian Ocean, the Philippines, Indonesia, and Micronesia. Of the estimated 17,000 square kilometers (6,600 square miles) of coral reef area in U.S. waters, only about 15 percent has been mapped in any detail. As a result, most management decisions affecting reef conservation and protection have been made without using them at all. By turning to satellite imagery, scientists have the opportunity to monitor changes caused by human and natural factors, setting the foundation for knowledgeable public policy recommendations on how to preserve them.

Surveying reefs from way up

Scientists attempted to study coral reefs by satellite imagery even before they began using IKONOS for this purpose. In April 1999, NASA and the U.S. Geological Survey (USGS) launched Landsat 7, a satellite that carried an instrument known as the Enhanced Thematic Mapper Plus (ETM+). The mission was for ETM+ to collect digital images of various areas of Earth from space. These images would become a resource for scientists studying issues related to agriculture, geology, forestry, regional planning, education, and national security. While planning this mission, NASA and USGS asked for feedback from scientists in the marine community on how Landsat 7 could help advance the study of coral reefs. Based on input received at that time, the satellite began regularly acquiring images of them.

There are, however, significant limitations to the usefulness of this imagery in studying coral reefs. Landsat 7, like other satellites before it, flies at a fixed position, looking straight down. At this constrained angle, the glare of sunlight reflected off the water's surface can at times be particularly unfavorable, making marine features impossible to observe. In addition, images taken by Landsat 7 are at lower resolution than those taken by IKONOS. In particular, color imagery from IKONOS can reveal objects as small as 4 meters (about 13 feet) across, while color imagery from Landsat 7 can show objects at a minimum width of 15 meters (about 49 feet).

Working with Rohmann and his team at NOAA, Space Imaging developed techniques to overcome the interference of the Sun's glare in the process of imaging by the IKONOS satellite. The satellite's camera was oriented in such a way that the reflection of sunlight from the ocean's surface was minimized and the penetration of light into the water was maximized. With this approach, crisp, high-resolution images of underwater features could be captured.

The uses of satellite images

The IKONOS satellite produces digital images that are both black-and-white and in color—particularly in the red, blue, and green wavelengths of the electromagnetic spectrum. The data captured in the green and blue bands are especially useful in allowing scientists to extract much information about the reef's makeup—information that would ordinarily require direct dives and other complex analyses to obtain. According to Rohmann's research, features as much as 30 meters (100 feet) below the surface can be seen in clear water using imagery captured by the 423-mile-high IKONOS satellite.

High-resolution satellite imagery may also prove useful for assessing the impact of hazardous material spills and ship groundings on coral reefs. [In 2000] a fishing boat ran aground on Pearl and Hermes Atoll, located more than 1,000 miles west of Honolulu in the northwestern Hawaiian Islands. Although an airport was available at Midway about 120 miles northwest, it was difficult to make arrangements to assess the damage done to the reef by the grounding.

The Pacific Ocean has many additional coral reef ecosystems that are much more remote than those associated with the Hawaiian Islands. There are hundreds of scattered islands and atolls that are so remote that a spill or grounding could go undetected or prove difficult to study even if reported. With access to high-resolution satellite imagery, scientists and managers now have a means to monitor and study these previously inaccessible areas.

The IKONOS satellite is providing the first imagery ever available for the shallow-water coral reef ecosystems of the northwestern Hawaiian Islands, where as much as 70 percent of the total reef area under direct U.S. protection is located. The data obtained are being analyzed by scientists at NOAA to generate the first classified maps of these reefs. Creating these maps is a crucial step in the process to designate this area as a National Marine Sanctuary, which will then become the second-largest marine protected area in the world, surpassed only by the Great Barrier Reef Marine Park of Australia.

From the work being done, the results indicate that high-resolution satellite imaging will be a highly useful technology for the quantitative mapping of reefs. Coordinating its work with universities and state and federal agencies in the United States and abroad, NOAA hopes to combine satellite imagery with information provided by the Geographic Information Systems to track the distribution of coral diseases, invasive species, and coral reef bleaching. The bleaching of reefs is a result of prolonged exposure to abnormally warm water temperatures that, for some parts of Earth, have been linked to weather patterns such as El Niño.[1]

NOAA is currently working with other government agencies to share the images collected, so they can be used for land-based conservation efforts as well. For example, the images are being successfully used to (1) monitor air pollution sources to better control air quality; (2) analyze runoff from mines to prevent heavy-metal seepage into mountain streams; and (3) study the introduction of grizzly bears into new habitats.

Reflecting on this progress, I find it rewarding to know that the technology being used is playing a vital role in helping protect fragile ecosystems. The discoveries being made will ensure that coral reefs, such as those I explored off the coast of Jamaica will have a better chance at survival and will still be around for my children and their children to visit and enjoy.

---

1. El Niño is a warming of the ocean surface off the western coast of South America that occurs every four to twelve years when upwelling of cold, nutrient-rich water does not occur. It causes die-offs of plankton and fish and affects Pacific jet stream winds, altering storm tracks and creating unusual weather patterns in various parts of the world.

13

Artificial Coral Reefs May Save Coral Ecosystems from Extinction

Caspar Henderson

Caspar Henderson is an environmental journalist and consultant whose articles have appeared in Ecologist, Environmental Finance, *and* New Scientist.

Artificial reefs may be the coral reefs of the future. Since the 1950s various refuse has been used to build artificial reefs in hopes of attracting fish and crustaceans. Structures have been built out of plastic, steel, and concrete but have failed to attract the marine life that natural coral reefs do. Now biologists are creating "Biorock," an artificial reef on which corals and other reef organisms seem to thrive. These artificial reefs are inexpensive to build and can handle ten times the stress that natural coral reefs can.

Far out in the Indian Ocean, on a rocky bank just beneath the waves, divers are growing a coral reef. Its skeleton—a framework of steel girders—sits on the seabed a few metres down. They swim around it, attaching small chunks of living coral to the girders with wire. Finally, one of them clips on an electrical cable that dangles from a raft floating above. Seconds later, tiny bubbles of hydrogen start to rise from the steel.

Creating a coral reef

They're making "Biorock." On board the raft is an array of so-lar cells and as the current generated flows through the metal frame, it triggers a chemical reaction in the seawater that coats the steel with a form of limestone that corals can't resist. Even-tually this metal structure should disappear beneath a multi-coloured forest of coral.

The experiment began in March [2002] at Saya de Malha, a bank on a submerged plateau in the western Indian Ocean, called the Mascarene Ridge. It was organised by marine biolo-gist Thomas Goreau and Wolf Hilbertz, an engineer and archi-tect, who have been growing artificial reefs all over the world for more than a decade.

Goreau and Hilbertz aren't the first to create artificial reefs, but they believe their structures are the best yet. Corals seem to love them, they're cheap to build and grow stronger as they age. And at a time when many reefs—and the creatures they support—are struggling to survive, these coral "arks" could pro-vide a lifeline for human communities that rely on the fish that reefs attract.

Goreau and Hilbertz even claim that corals growing on their artificial reefs are over 10 times as likely to survive stress-ful environmental changes as naturally formed coral. If they're right, these structures may be one of the few remaining hopes for saving much of the world's coral from extinction.

Coral reefs under assault

This has never been more important: reefs all over the planet are under massive assault. The Global Coral Reef Monitoring Network, based in Australia, estimates that more than a quar-ter of the world's reefs have died in the past few decades and that at least another quarter will perish within twenty years.

The assaults take several forms, including physical destruc-tion caused by fishing and pollution by nutrients leached into the sea from farmland and cities. But global warming looks set to be the gravest threat of all.

Coral polyps feed on food particles in the water, and as they grow they deposit calcium carbonate around themselves to form a protective skeleton. The polyps also capture energy from sunlight, courtesy of photosynthetic algae called zooxan-thellae embedded in their outer surfaces. It's the algae that give corals their bright colours. But they are sensitive to small rises in seawater temperature: an increase of just 1° Celsius somehow forces them out of the polyps, leaving the coral with a "bleached" appearance. Without the energy the algae provide, the coral often dies.

> **//** *Since the 1950s artificial reefs have been built from refuse such as scrap metal and car tires in the hope of increasing yields of fish and crustaceans.* **//**

Mass bleaching is becoming a regular event. In 1998, for example, warm seawater killed most corals in the Indian Ocean. Then, in 2002, corals across the South Pacific died, with Australia's Great Barrier Reef hit especially hard. "There is little doubt that current rates of warming in tropical seas will lead to longer and more intense bleaching events," says Ove Hoegh-Guldberg of the Centre for Marine Studies at the University of Queensland, Australia, who chairs the UN Working Group on Coral Bleaching.

Now there's a new threat. As levels of carbon dioxide in the atmosphere rise, the concentration of the gas in seawater is rising too, and researchers believe that this may prevent polyps building their skeletons.

Artificial reefs may save the day

Could artificial reefs save the day? Not traditional designs, says Goreau. Since the 1950s artificial reefs have been built from refuse such as scrap metal and car tires in the hope of increasing yields of fish and crustaceans. More recently, structures have been built from plastic, steel and concrete, but most remain relatively barren compared with natural reefs.

Biorock reefs, on the other hand, are rather more sophisticated. The concept dates back to the mid-1970s when Hilbertz, working at the University of Texas at Austin, tried using electrodes immersed in seawater to mimic the way seashells and reefs grow.

Electrolysed water and bubbles of hydrogen form at the cathode as electrons bind to hydrogen ions in the seawater. To compensate for the loss of these ions, carbonic acid (H_2CO_3) in the seawater around the cathode breaks down, releasing hydrogen ions and carbonate ions. Hilbertz noticed that when the carbonate ions reach a critical concentration, a form of limestone made primarily from calcium carbonate, called aragonite, is deposited on the cathode.

He also found that brucite a mineral made from magnesium hydroxide forms at the cathode. This is softer than aragonite, so to build useful structures, he had to find ways to strengthen the material. Hilbertz discovered he could eliminate the brucite by adjusting the current and by periodically turning it off completely, giving the more soluble brucite a chance to dissolve. The result was a metal cathode coated with a material as strong as concrete. He also found that the best anode was a titanium mesh covered with a layer of ruthenium oxide, which is resistant to corrosion underwater.

Hilbertz reasoned that if you generated the electricity from renewable resources such as solar power, you could create low-cost limestone "reefs" of any shape and size. In experiments, he found he could grow the coatings at up to 5 centimetres a year. The structures would require little maintenance and would even heal themselves when damaged. And since the limestone resembles natural reefs, coral should colonise it rapidly.

Finding no ill effects

However, some marine scientists worried that electrolysis might damage living coral. So Hilbertz began experiments to determine what the effects might be. He attached Elkhorn coral to two steel structures in seawater and passed a small electric current through one but not the other. "Nothing remarkable took place on the control," he says. "In contrast, corals thrived on the electrolysed structure."

To his surprise, the results were ignored. Then in 1988, Goreau, a Jamaican marine biologist researching coral growth in the Caribbean, read of Hilbertz's work and got in touch. Together they have spent over a decade working together with the Global Coral Reef Alliance (GCRA), an umbrella organisation dedicated to protecting coral reefs, to construct Biorock reefs around the world.

Typically, each structure is built from a dome-shaped steel frame up to 12 metres across, and costs about $1000 to construct. The largest so far, one of seven in the Maldives, is 40 metres long and 8 metres wide. And at Pemuteran, on the Indonesian Island of Bali, they have Installed 22 structures, with a total length of 220 metres.

The amount of electrical power required by each Biorock reef is low. A structure of 100 square metres, for example, requires less than 300 watts to grow. Most reefs built to date take their power from arrays of solar cells, either on shore or aboard a raft floating nearby, but Goreau is also considering using power generated by tidal turbines attached to the seabed.

Coral reefs get a boost

Most importantly, the variety of creatures living on and around these structures after a few years seems to match that of natural reefs. "The corals [on the Biorock reefs at Pemuteran] are clearly doing well," says Steve Oakley, an environmental scientist at the Tropical Research and Conservation Centre based in Kuching in Malaysia. "There's good fish diversity, and certainly many more fish on that stretch of reef than others nearby."

> *Researchers believe that the corals on their reefs are more resistant to environmental pressures such as pollution and global warming than natural systems.*

In fact, the researchers believe that the corals on their reefs are more resistant to environmental pressures such as pollution and global warming than natural systems. Without needing to use as much of their own energy to create a calcareous skeleton, each coral polyp can put more energy into growth and reproduction, and this seems to make them better at withstanding stress. Goreau and Hilbertz estimate that coral growth on Biorock is 3 or 4 times as fast as on ordinary rock, and the ability of these corals to survive events that kill most corals on natural reefs is striking. "In most parts of the Maldives, for example, less than 5 per cent of corals survived the catastrophic bleaching of 1998," says Goreau. "On our Biorock structures, more than 80 per cent of corals not only survived, they flourished."

Spurred on by these results, Goreau and Hilbertz want to grow small coral gardens just tens or hundreds of square metres in size that could help protect coral reef systems from the threat of global warming. And they hope that a network of these "arks" could ultimately be used to recolonise large areas where coral has died. "Coral nurseries are the only way to keep corals from extinction," says Seferino Smith, operations manager at Sapibenega Kuna Lodge, an eco-resort owned by the Ukupseni community of Kuna Yala in Panama. Here, local groups are working with GCRA to build Biorock nurseries to support both fisheries and tourism. "We should multiply these nurseries all over the Kuna reserve and around the world," says Smith.

However, some questions remain. No one yet knows how rising levels of CO_2 in seawater will affect the rate of growth of coral on Biorock. An artificial reef is also unlikely to exactly duplicate a natural one, Goreau admits. Small differences will alter the balance of ecological competitiveness between reef organisms, he says, so the final make-up of creatures may differ. And voracious predators—the coral-eating snail *Drupella* and the crown of thorns starfish *Acanthaster*, for example—remain a formidable challenge. In the past, these starfish have caused serious damage to Australia's Great Barrier Reef, for example.

Some experts have yet to be convinced that these reefs offer all the advantages that their creators claim. To prove that Hilbertz and Goreau's idea is solid, other reef scientists will have to see the hard data, says Hoegh-Guldberg. "I certainly don't want to dismiss it at this stage. It is a very interesting approach."

Fans of Biorock are the first to acknowledge that more research is needed. Just why the process increases the rate of coral growth and creates healthier animals isn't fully understood, says Cody Shwaiko, founder and head of the Komodo Foundation, an Indonesian conservation and community development charity. "[There needs to be] more work, experimenting with parameters in a controlled environment in order to better understand the process," she says. Goreau agrees, and the GCRA is working with Shwaiko to establish a research programme in Indonesia. Goreau and Hilbertz are also interested in using Biorock as the foundations for seawalls, breakwaters and jetties, estimating that it could be a tenth as expensive as equivalent concrete structures, making it ideal for use by developing nations threatened with rising sea levels.

Organizations to Contact

The editors have compiled the following list of organizations concerned with the issues debated in this book. The descriptions are derived from materials provided by the organizations. All have publications or information available for interested readers. The list was compiled on the date of publication of the present volume; the information provided here may change. Be aware that many organizations take several weeks or longer to respond to inquiries, so allow as much time as possible.

Center for Coastal Studies (CCS)
Texas A&M University, Corpus Christi Natural Resources Center
6300 Ocean Dr., Suite 3200, Corpus Christi, TX 78412
(361) 825-2736 • fax: (361) 825-2770
e-mail: jtunnell@falcon.tamucc.edu
Web site: www.sci.tamucc.edu/ccs/welcome.html

CCS, an interdisciplinary marine research institute, conducts basic and applied research, ecological monitoring, public education outreach, and graduate-level education and research programs. Its main focus is on marine topics concerning the Texas coast, Gulf of Mexico, and the wider Caribbean. Selected articles and reports are available on its Web site, including *Porewater Toxicity Testing: A Novel Approach for Assessing Contaminant Impacts in the Vicinity of Coral Reefs* and *Effects of Light Availability on Reef Community Structure of Hermatypic Corals Within Sian Ka'an Biosphere Reserve, Quintana Roo, Mexico.*

Coral Cay Conservation (CCC)
125 High St., Colliers Wood, London SW19 2JG UK
+44 (0) 870 750 0668 • fax: +44 (0) 870 750 0667
e-mail: lg@coralcay.org • Web site: www.coralcay.org

CCC, a not-for-profit international conservation organization, helps protect threatened coral reefs by sending teams of volunteers to survey some of the world's most endangered coral reefs. CCC publishes *The Reef and Leaf*, a quarterly newsletter. A bibliography and CCC papers, reports, conference proceedings, and presentations are available on its Web site.

Cousteau Society
710 Settlers Landing Rd., Hampton, VA 23669
(757) 722-9300 • fax: (757) 722-8185
e-mail: cousteau@cousteausociety.org
Web site: www.cousteausociety.org

The Cousteau Society's mission is to educate people to understand, love, and protect the water systems of the planet, marine and freshwater, for the well-being of future generations. Its Web site provides news articles and fact sheets, including "Mangroves Make More Fish," an article highlighting the importance of mangrove forests to increasing the biomass of coral reef fish. Viewable videos of Cousteau team expeditions are also available on its Web site.

Earthwatch Institute
680 Mt. Auburn St., Watertown, MA 02272
(800) 776-0188 • (617) 926-8200 • fax: (617) 926-8532
e-mail: info@earthwatch.org • Web site: www.earthwatch.org

Earthwatch Institute engages people worldwide in scientific field research and education to promote the understanding and action necessary for a sustainable environment. Earthwatch offers various grants and fellowships and worldwide short-term voluntary expeditions to assist scientists in their research. Its Web site publishes numerous articles, bibliographies, photos, and maps and provides links to other Web sites.

Environmental Defense
5655 College Ave., Oakland, CA 94618
(510) 658-8008 ext. 226 • fax: (510) 658-0630
e-mail: info@environmentaldefense.org
Web site: www.environmentaldefense.org

Environmental Defense is a leading national nonprofit organization whose mission is to protect human health, restore our oceans and ecosystems, and curb global warming. Its Web site publishes news reports, fact sheets, and publications, including *A Search for the Truth: Impacts of the Executive Orders Establishing the Northwestern Hawaiian Islands Coral Reef Ecosystem Reserve in the Context of the "Review" of the Executive Orders* and *Mangroves Enhance the Biomass of Coral Reef Fish Communities in the Caribbean.* An extensive audio/video library is also available on its Web site.

Global Coral Reef Alliance (GCRA)
37 Pleasant St., Cambridge, MA 02139
(617) 864-4226 • (617) 864-0433
e-mail: goreau@bestweb.net • Web site: www.globalcoral.org

GCRA is a small, nonprofit organization dedicated to growing, protecting, and managing the most threatened of all marine ecosystems—coral reefs. A coalition of volunteer scientists, divers, environmentalists, and other individuals and organizations, GCRA is committed to coral reef preservation. Its Web site publishes news releases, articles, and papers covering a variety of coral reef issues, including *A Strategy for Restoration of Damaged Coral Reefs and Fisheries at Ashton Harbour, Union Island, the Grenadines* and *The Biorock™ Process Accelerates Coral Growth.*

International Coral Reef Information Network (ICRIN)
Coral Reef Alliance
417 Montgomery St., Suite 205, San Francisco, CA 94104
(415) 834-0900 • fax: (415) 834-0999
e-mail: icrin@coral.org • Web site: www.coralreef.org

ICRIN is a communications and information project of the International Coral Reef Action Network (ICRAN) and the International Coral Reef Initiative (ICRI). ICRIN publishes general coral reef information, provides coral reef outreach tools and resources, and serves as a central coral reef communications and network hub. ICRIN publishes a quarterly newsletter, *ICRI News*, and the report *Coral Reefs at Risk*, which are available on its Web site. The Web site also offers the Education and Outreach Library, an extensive database of coral reef materials gathered from organizations all over the world, an international directory of coral reef organizations, and a photo bank.

International Society for Reef Studies (ISRS)
Dauphin Island Sea Lab
101 Bienville Blvd., Dauphin Island, AL 36528
e-mail: smiller@gate.net • Web site: www.fit.edu/isrs/

ISRS promotes the production and dissemination of scientific knowledge and understanding of coral reefs. ISRS offers members free subscriptions to *Coral Reefs* and *Reef Encounter*. Its Web site publishes reports and briefs, including *Coral Reefs and Climate Change*, and links to other coral reef Web sites.

Natural Resources Defense Council (NRDC)
40 West Twentieth St., New York, NY 10011
(212) 727-2700 • fax: (212) 727-1773
e-mail: nrdcinfo@nrdc.org • Web site: www.nrdc.org

NRDC has the support of more than 1 million members and online activists whose goal is to protect the planet's wildlife and wild places and to ensure a safe and healthy environment for all living things. NRDC publishes the magazines *On Earth, Nature's Voice: The Bulletin of Environmental Campaigns and Victories*, and *The Green Life*. Press releases on environmental legislation, articles, and reports are available on its Web site. The Web site also publishes a glossary of environmental terms and a list of major federal laws pertaining to the environment.

Ocean Conservancy
1725 DeSales St. NW, Suite 600, Washington, DC 20036
(202) 429-5609
e-mail: info@oceanconservancy.org
Web site: www.oceanconservancy.org

The Ocean Conservancy is committed to protecting ocean environments and conserving the global abundance and diversity of marine life. Its Condition Monitoring Program (RECON) trains recreational divers to observe and record information about selected coral reefs. The conservancy publishes the *Blue Planet Quarterly* and the annual *Health of the Oceans Report*. The Web site publishes articles on ocean issues and conservation and action alerts on current marine policies.

Reef Check Foundation
Institute of the Environment
1362 Hershey Hall, 95-1496
University of California at Los Angeles, Los Angeles, CA 90095-1496
(310) 794-4985 • fax: (310) 825-0758
e-mail: rcheck@ucla.edu • Web site: www.reefcheck.org

Reef Check works with communities, governments, and businesses to scientifically monitor, restore, and maintain coral reef health. The Reef Check Web site offers various publications, including *Marine Aquarium Trade Coral Reef Protocol (MAQTRAC)* and *The Global Coral Reef Crisis:*

Trends and Solutions. Current and back issues of its newsletter, *The Transect Line*, and links to current news articles, government sites, organizations, and reference material are also available on its Web site.

Reef Relief
201 William St., PO Box 430, Key West, FL 33040
(305) 294-3100 • fax: (305) 293-9515
e-mail: reef@bellsouth.net • Web site: www.reefrelief.org

Reef Relief is a grassroots, nonprofit coral reef organization dedicated to preserving and protecting living coral reef ecosystems through local, regional, and international efforts. Its Web site publishes *Reef Line*, a quarterly newsletter, and provides over four hundred documents and scientific studies on protecting the coral reefs, including *Indian Ocean Could Lose Coral Islands in 50 Years* and *Death and Resurrection on Caribbean Reefs.*

San Diego Oceans Foundation (SDOF)
PO Box 90672, San Diego, CA 92169-2672
(619) 523-1903
e-mail: sdoceans@sdoceans.org • Web site: www.sdoceans.org

SDOF is a nonprofit community organization devoted to promoting ocean stewardship through community-supported projects that enhance the ocean habitat and encourage sustainable use of the ocean's resources. SDOF supports scientific research, fisheries enhancement, science, education, pollution prevention, and habitat enhancement. SDOF publishes a biannual newsletter, *Ocean Waves*. Its Web site has reports that focus on research, education, conservation, and habitat enhancement and links to other marine Web sites.

United Nations Environment Programme
World Conservation Monitoring Centre (UNEP-WCMC)
219 Huntingdon Rd., Cambridge CB3 0DL UK
+44 (0)1223 277314 • fax: +44 (0)1223 277136
e-mail: info@unep-wcmc.org • Web site: www.unep-wcmc.org

UNEP-WCMC is the world biodiversity information and assessment center of the UN Environment Programme. The center's activities include assessment and early warning studies in forest, dryland, freshwater, and marine ecosystems. UNEP-WCMC publications include *The World Atlas of Coral Reefs* and *Global Trade in Coral*. The UNEP-WCMC Web site provides a searchable database of environmental issues, international agreements, and maps of coral reefs.

World Resources Institute (WRI)
10 G St. NE, Suite 800, Washington, DC 20002
(202) 729-7600 • fax: (202) 729-7610
e-mail: gregm@wri.org • Web site: www.wri.org

WRI is an independent, nonprofit organization with a staff of more than one hundred scientists, economists, policy experts, business analysts, statistical analysts, mapmakers, and communicators working to protect the earth and improve people's lives. The WRI Web site publishes reports, including *Reefs at Risk: A Map-based Indicator of Threats to the World's Coral Reefs* and *Reefs at Risk in Southeast Asia*. Earth Trends, the Web site's searchable database, contains maps, country profiles, features, and data tables.

World Wildlife Fund (WWF)
1250 Twenty-fourth St. NW, Washington, DC 20037-1175
(202) 861-8301 • fax: (202) 293-9211
e-mail: hr@wwfus.org • Web site: www.panda.org

WWF's mission is to stop the degradation of the planet's natural environment and to build a future in which humans live in harmony with nature by conserving the world's biological diversity, ensuring that the use of renewable natural resources is sustainable, and promoting the reduction of pollution and wasteful consumption. The WWF Web site publishes fact sheets, current news, and articles, including "The Implications of Climate Change for Australia's Great Barrier Reef."

Bibliography

Books

Dirk Bryant et al. *Reefs at Risk: A Map-based Indicator of Threats to the World's Coral Reefs.* Washington, DC: World Resources Institute, 1998.

Melissa S. Cole *Wild Marine Habitats: Coral Reefs.* San Diego: Blackbirch Press, 2004.

Osha Gray Davidson *The Enchanted Braid: Coming to Terms with Nature on the Coral Reef.* New York: John Wiley, 1998.

Stephen Harrigan *Water and Light: A Diver's Journey to a Coral Reef.* Austin: University of Texas Press, 1999.

T.R. McClanahan, ed. *Coral Reefs of the Indian Ocean: Their Ecology and Conservation.* New York: Oxford University Press, 2000.

Richard C. Murphy *Coral Reefs: Cities Under the Sea.* Princeton, NJ: Darwin Press, 2002.

Linda M. Pitkin *Coral Fish.* Washington, DC: Smithsonian Institution Press, 2001.

Greg Pyers *Coral Reef Explorer.* Austin: Raintree, 2004.

Reef Check Foundation *Reef Check's Five Year Report—Trends and Solutions: The Coral Reef Crisis.* Los Angeles: Reef Check Foundation, 2002.

Peter F. Sale *Coral Reef Fishes: Dynamics and Diversity in a Complex Ecosystem.* San Diego: Academic Press, 2002.

Jan Sapp *What Is Natural? Coral Reef Crisis.* New York: Oxford University Press, 1999.

Charles Sheppard *Coral Reefs: Ecology, Threats, and Conservation.* Stillwater, MN: Voyageur Press, 2002.

George D. Stanley, ed. *The History and Sedimentology of Ancient Reef Systems.* Dordrecht, Netherlands: Kluwer Academic, 2001.

Roger Steene *Coral Seas.* Willowdale, Ontario: Firefly Books, 1998.

Salvatore Tocci *Coral Reefs: Life Below the Sea.* Danbury, CT: Franklin Watts, 2004.

Eric Wolanski *Oceanographic Processes of Coral Reefs: Physical and Biological Links in the Great Barrier Reef.* Maryknoll, NY: Orbis, 2000.

Periodicals

Neville Coleman — "Don't Shoot the Messenger (Threats to Coral Ecosystems)," *Wildlife Australia*, Summer 2001.

Neville Coleman — "Oil and the Great Barrier Reef," *Ecologist*, October 2001.

Communications Today — "Gov. Bush Set to OK Cable Corridors Despite Findings," June 27, 2003.

Economist — "What Price Coral?" November 4, 2000.

Environment — "Ghostly Coral—Ravages of El Niño Can Be Seen in the Corals Along the Coasts Around the World," January 2001.

J. Gorman — "Biodiversity Hot Spots: Top Ten Sea Locales Make Sobering List," *Science News*, February 16, 2002.

Sharon Guynup — "Australia's Great Barrier Reef," *Science World*, September 4, 2000.

Paul Haynos — "Cool Coral," *Environment*, April 2003.

Paul Haynos — "Coral Layers May Reveal Climate Cycles," *Environment*, March 2003.

Caspar Henderson — "Coral Decline," *Ecologist*, February 2001.

Jeffrey Kluger — "Coral Reefs Hang On—in Spite of It All," *Time*, August 25, 2003.

S. Milius — "Film Solves Mystery of Sleepwalking Coral," *Science News*, January 13, 2001.

S. Milius — "Near-Sterile Hybrids Boost Coral Diversity," *Science News*, June 15, 2002.

Henry Lee Morgenstern — "Clouds over the Coral," *E: The Environmental Magazine*, March 1, 1999.

Britt Norlander — "Coral Crisis! Humans Are Killing Off These Bustling Underwater Cities. Can Coral Reefs Be Saved?" *Science World*, December 8, 2003.

Janet Raloff — "Aircraft Spies on Health of Coral Reefs," *Science News*, September 8, 2001.

Janet Raloff — "Wanted: Reef Cleaners," *Science News*, August 25, 2001.

Kate Rope — "Sunken Treasures," *Mother Jones*, May/June 1998.

Soames Summerhayes — "Rescuing Reefs in Hot Water: Amid Worldwide Collapses of Coral Reefs Comes Hope in a Simple Discovery," *Nature Conservancy*, Fall 2002.

David Taylor — "Fishing for the Truth," *Rodale's Scuba Diving*, July 2001.

Pete Taylor

"Spectacular Conception—Deep Within the Gulf of Mexico, an Annual Nighttime Spectacle Is Providing Scientists with New Clues to Coral Conservation," *National Wildlife*, October 1, 2000.

Julia Whitty

"Shoals of Time," *Harper's*, January 2001.

Web Sites

NOAA's Coral Reef Information System (CoRIS)

www.coris.noaa.gov. The National Oceanic and Atmospheric Association's (NOAA's) Coral Reef Information System (CoRIS) provides access to NOAA data and facts about coral reefs. The Web site's library maintains a comprehensive collection of articles, essays, and reports on coral reefs, a searchable database, and links to other Web sites.

Reefbase

www.reefbase.org. Reefbase is an Internet repository of information on coral reefs worldwide. It provides information on the status, quantity, and types of coral reefs in 131 countries. Reefbase reports information on threats to individual coral reefs, which reefs are at risk and which are protected, current legislation, and what is being done to alleviate the problems. The Web site includes custom-made maps, photos, an extensive bibliography of over 20,695 coral reef–related publications, printable articles, and links to other Web sites.

Reefnet

www.reefnet.org. Reefnet is an Internet information service that provides articles from top researchers and scientists on the latest coral reef research and scientific discoveries. Reefnet also reports on topics discussed at coral reef symposiums, including conservation and management strategies of coral reefs worldwide.

Index

adsorbents, 46
Africa, 56–57, 74
African dust
  agriculture and, 56–57
  composition of, 62
  coral reef diseases and, 58–61
  damages Caribbean coral reefs, 56,
    81–82
  impact upon human beings, 63–64
  other coral reef deterioration
    factors and, 64
  pesticides and, 63–64
  radiation and, 63
agribusiness. *See* agriculture;
  international trade
agricultural run-off, 21–22, 62
  see also pesticides; pollution
agriculture, 11, 19, 20, 21–22, 37
  see also African dust; pesticides;
    pollution; run-off; sedimentation
algae, 35, 57, 88
Ansula, A., 45
Apo Reef, 46–47
aquaculture, 55
  see also mariculture ponds
aquariums, collecting for, 12, 14–15,
  31
  see also coral reef(s), organisms;
    fishing, cyanide
artificial coral reefs, 93–98
Aspergillus, 60
Australia, 19–25, 53–54, 80
  see also Great Barrier Reef
Australian Institute of Marine
  Science (AIMS), 20, 57

Baker, Andrew, 8–9
Baker, D. James, 82–83
Baliunas, Sallie, 33
Barbor, Charles Victor, 48
Best, Barbara, 10
Biological Resources Program (World
  Resources Institute), 48
Biorock, 93, 94, 97–98
Bjorndal, Karen A., 79
Black Band (coral disease), 41, 45
Blair, S.M., 32–43
bleaching. *See* coral bleaching
Boat Owners Association of the
  United States, 81
bombs, 13–14

Bruckner, Andrew W., 69
Bunkley-Williams, Lucy, 57

California, 80
Cameron, A.M., 41
Cane, Mark A., 35–36
carbon dioxide, 37–38
Caribbean monk seal, 78
Caribbean Sea, 57–58, 60–61, 79, 87
Causey, Billy, 64
chemicals, 37
  see also pesticides; poisons;
    pollution
Clinton, Bill, 85, 89
Coastal Resource Assessment
  Training, 39
Colgan, M.W., 41
Collins, Tom, 7
commercial fishing, 13–15
  see also aquariums, collecting for;
    fishing, cyanide
Commonwealth Scientific and
  Industrial Research Organisation
  (CSIRO), 27
conservation measures. *See* coral
  reef(s), conservation efforts for
construction, 44
consumer awareness, 17–18
consumer trade, 69–76
containment booms, 46
Convention on the International
  Trade in Endangered Species of
  Wild Fauna and Flora (CITES), 15
coral bleaching
  Caribbean area and, 58
  causes of, 12, 29–30
  live coral harvesting and, 73
  threatens coral reefs, 28, 41–42,
    94–95
  con, 33–38
"Coral Bleaching, Coral Mortality,
  and Global Climate Change" (U.S.
  State Department), 31–32
coral diseases, 41–42, 58–61
  see also coral bleaching
coral polyps, 35
coral predators, 40–42
coral reef(s)
  animal and plant species supported
    by, 11
  are not threatened, 34–35

conservation efforts for
  education programs and, 46–47
  national monitoring system and,
    83
  Philippines, 74–75
  United States, 75–76
as critical habitat for fish, 78–79
damage to, natural and human,
  39–47
destruction of, in Caribbean, 56–64
deterioration worldwide, 89
developing countries and, 10–11
diseases, 11, 41–42, 58–61
financial resources and, 10–11
fishing practices impact, 13–16
as food providers, 11
importance of, 11, 28–29, 87–88
locations of, 10–11
medical potential of, 8–9
organisms, 69–76
sea levels and, 31
skeletons, 14
statistics, 7, 11, 12, 65–66
threats to, 9, 10, 11–12, 42–43, 88
Coral Reef Task Force, 75–76, 81–82
crown-of-thorns starfish, 9, 23, 37,
  40–41, 45
cyanide, 6, 13, 15
  see also fishing, cyanide

Davidson, Keay, 77
decompression sickness, 50
deep-water disposal, 46
deforestation, 44
development. *See* construction
diseases. *See* coral reef(s), diseases
Dollar, S.J., 42, 43, 45, 46

earthquakes, 42, 43
economic factors, 69–76, 84
  see also international trade
educational programs, 46
El Niño, 29, 35, 42, 43, 59, 65–66
endangered species, 15
Endean, R., 41
English, Brian J., 39
Enhanced Thematic Mapper Plus
  (ETM+), 90
Erdmann, M.V., 52
Evans, Michael, 35–36
Executive Order for the Protection of
  Coral Reefs, 16, 32, 71
explosives, 13–14, 37, 46–47, 55
extinction, of species, 78, 93–98

Fenical, William, 8
fertilizer, 55
  see also African dust; agriculture;

sedimentation
Fiji, 72
fishing, 11, 12, 16
  commercial, 13–15
  cyanide, 48–51
    consumer responsibility and, 54
    consumer risk and, 51–52
    deleterious effects of, 52
    destroys reef life, 69
    government policy and, 54–55
    is destructive to coral reefs, 51–52,
      73–74
    statistics, 53
  dynamite, 13–14, 46–47, 55
  excessive, 14–15, 37, 55, 79, 84
fishing bans, 77–80, 81–85
Florida, 42–43, 64
Florida Keys National Marine
  Sanctuary, 64
forestry, 13
fortified dust, 61–63
  see also African dust
fossil fuels, 32, 37–38
Furnas, Miles, 20

Garrison, Ginger, 58, 59–62
Geographic Information Systems, 92
Geophysical Research Letters, 58
Global Coral Reef Alliance (GCRA),
  97–98
Global Coral Reef Monitoring
  Network, 89, 94
global warming
  causes coral bleaching, 22–23, 26–32
    con, 33–38
  El Niño and, 29–30
  Great Barrier Reef and, 22–23
  human-induced, 36–37
  Kyoto Protocol and, 37–38
  statistics, 29
Goreau, Thomas, 94, 96–98
grasshoppers, 59
Great Barrier Reef
  agriculture is destructive to, 20–21
    con, 21–22
  cyanide effects on, 51–52
  El Niño and, 43
  fish catch record studies involving,
    79
  importance of, 20–21
  is not threatened, 19–25
  mapping of, 90
  monitoring for damage, 20
  tourism and, 80
  water quality reporting, 24–25
Great Barrier Reef Marine Park, 21,
  22, 92
Great Pacific Climate Shift of

1976–1977, 36
greenhouse gases, 31, 32
Greenpeace, 22, 24, 26
Grigg, R.W., 42, 43, 45, 46

Hawaii, 12, 43, 74, 92
Hayes, Marshall, 62
Henderson, Caspar, 93
Hierta, E., 46
Hilbertz, Wolf, 94, 96, 97–98
Hinrichsen, D., 47
Hoegh-Guldberg, Ove, 22, 24–25, 26, 95, 98
hooka rig, 16
hurricanes, 42–43

IKONOS (satellite), 89, 90–92
Indian Ocean, 93, 94–95
Indonesia, 13, 43–54, 71, 97, 98
Infectious Disease Review (journal), 57
International Coral Reef Symposium (ICRS), 60
International Marinelife Alliance (IMA), 48, 52–53, 75
international trade
   aquarium-fish-collection statistics, 15
   in coral reef
      live fish, 53–54
      organisms, 69–76
      products, 88
   Kyoto Protocol and, 37–38
   tourism and, 28–29
   U.S. should be responsible in, 16–17
International Year of the Coral Reef, 47

Jackson, Jerome, 37
Johannes, R.E., 52

Kirk, Mark, 37
Komodo Foundation, 98
Kyoto Protocol, 37–38

Landsat 7 (satellite), 90–91
land use, 11, 19
   see also agriculture; forestry
La Niña, 35, 65–66
Latin America, 60–61, 97
Lessios, Harilaos, 61
Lindsay Reef, 36
Linsley, Braddock D., 36
live coral harvesting, 72–73
live reef fishing trade, 53–55, 73–74
locusts, 59, 63–64
logging, 44
Lough, Janice, 43

low tides, 44
Lydecker, Ryck, 81

Maldives, 98
mangrove forests, 13, 55
mariculture ponds, 13
Marine Aquarium Council (MAC), 75
marine
   ornamental trade, 14–15
   protected areas, 37, 84–85
   replenishment zones, 82
   reserves, 84–85
   wilderness areas, 82
   see also coral reef(s), conservation efforts for; fishing bans; "no-take zones"
Marshall, Paul, 24
Mascarene Ridge, 94
Max Planck Institute (MPI), 27
McAllister, D.E., 45
McGrath, Thomas A., 36
McIntosh, T.L., 42–43
minerals, 96
   see also African dust
mining, 31, 44
monk seal, 78
Moore, Franklin, 10
Mostkoff, B.J., 42–43
Mozambique, 74

National Action Plan to Conserve Coral Reefs, 82
National Aeronautic and Space Administration (NASA), 90
National Cancer Institute (NCI), 9
National Marine Fisheries Service, 83
National Marine Sanctuary, 2
National Oceanic and Atmospheric Administration (NOAA), 9, 44, 83, 86, 87, 92
North Atlantic Oscillation (NAO), 58–59
North Pacific, 36
"no-take zones," 77–80, 83–84
Nowak, Rachel, 19
Nussman, Mike, 84–85

Oakley, Steve, 97
ocean temperature. *See* global warming
oil drilling, 31, 45–46
oil spills, 46
overfertilizing, 45
oxidation, 62

Pacific Decadal Oscillation, 36
   see also El Niño; global warming
Paerl, Hans, 62

Pandolfi, John, 78, 79–80
pesticides, 21, 22, 55, 63–64
pet industry, 14–15
Pet-Soede, L., 52
Philippines, 13, 46–47, 52–53, 73–74, 88
phytoplankton, 45
poisons, 6, 13, 16
  see also cyanide; fishing, cyanide
pollution, 45–46, 88
  see also greenhouse gases
population, 11
Pratt, Vaughan R., 48
Prospero, Joseph, 58–59, 63

red dust. See African dust
red tide, 41–42
Richardson, L.L., 41, 45
Ridd, Peter, 20, 21–22, 24
Riepen, M., 52
Rohmann, Steve, 87, 89
run-off, 11, 37, 43, 44, 62
  see also agricultural run-off
Ryan, John C., 56

Sala, Enric, 78, 79
satellite imaging, 86–92
Saya de Malha, 94
Schrag, Daniel P., 36
sedimentation, 21–22, 31, 40, 44–45, 68
Seven Wonders: Everyday Things for a Healthier Planet (Ryan), 56
sewage, 46, 67–68
Shinn, Gene, 58, 59, 63, 64
shrimp production, 13
Shwaiko, Cody, 98
siltation. See sedimentation
Smith, Garnet, 59–69
Smith, Garriet W., 36
Smith, Seferino, 97
Smithsonian Tropical Research Institute, 61
Soliday, Brian, 86
Soon, Willie, 33
Spalding, Mark, 34
Status of Coral Reefs of the World 2000

(Wilkinson), 57
storms, 42–43
Szmant, Alina, 62–63, 64

Tanguisson Reef, 41
technology solutions, 46
tides, 43, 44
tourism
  African dust and, 64
  coral reef organisms and, 28–29, 39, 88
  impact on, by reef and beach condition, 28–29
  as threat to coral reefs, 39, 55, 65–68
Tropical Research and Conservation Center, 97

United Nations Environment Programme (UNEP), 34, 65
United Nations Working Group on Coral Bleaching, 95
United States, 16–18, 69–70, 71, 83
U.S. Agency for International Development (USAID), 10, 18
U.S. Geological Survey (USGS), 58, 59, 90
U.S. State Department, 31

volcanic eruptions, 42, 43, 63

weather, 42–43
Weir, Julianna, 60
Wellington, Gerard M., 36
White Band (coral disease), 41, 45
Wilkinson, Clive, 23, 45–46, 57
Williams, David, 21
Williams, Ernest, 57
World Resources Institute (WRI), 48
Worldwatch Institute, 56
World Wildlife Fund (WWF), 24

Yellow Band (coral disease), 41, 45

zooxanthellae, 29, 41–42
  see also coral bleaching